The Most Bea Suicide,

The Story of

Evelyn McHale

By

Wayne J. Gombar

Prologue:

The Stillness After the Fall

The sirens had not yet reached the block when Robert Wiles raised his camera. A crowd had gathered, shoes scraping on the pavement, voices hushed to whispers that sounded strangely reverent. There, on the crumpled roof of a black United Nations limousine, lay the figure of a young woman. Her gloved hands folded neatly over her chest, pearls resting just above the torn collar of her blouse, she might have been sleeping if not for the twisted wreck of metal beneath her.

Wiles was only a student, not yet hardened by the demands of professional news photography.

His fingers trembled as he focused, but his eye was steady. He understood—instinctively—that the world would remember this image. He clicked the shutter, sealing Evelyn McHale's final moment into history. Later, his photograph would be called "the most beautiful suicide," as though tragedy could be framed in the language of aesthetics. But in that instant, before the words and myths, there was only the silence of a city holding its breath.

Above them, the Empire State Building loomed, its spire reaching into a pale May sky. Tourists still crowded its observation deck, unaware of the drama unfolding far below. For Evelyn, the building had not been a monument of triumph but a stage for escape. The tallest tower in the world became, in her final choice, a paradox: a symbol of America's postwar confidence and of one woman's private despair.

To those who stood in the street that day, she seemed peaceful—serene, even. But peace was not what had driven her from the 86th floor. It was fear, and weariness, and the weight of a future she could not inhabit.

Her fiancé, Barry Rhodes, would later tell police he had no warning. They had kissed goodbye only days earlier in Pennsylvania, and she had promised to see him again. Yet Evelyn's farewell note betrayed another truth: "He is much better off without me. I wouldn't make a good wife for anybody."

What life had brought her to this sentence? What shadows lingered in her past, what storms gathered in her thoughts during those final hours? She was twenty-three years old, with her whole future arranged before her—marriage, stability, a household of her own—yet she recoiled from it as though it were a cage. The city around her hummed with ambition, skyscrapers rising, veterans returning home, women pressed between wartime independence and postwar obedience. Evelyn was caught in that current, pushed toward a life prescribed by others, until the pull of the void seemed gentler than the demands of tomorrow.

In the photograph, Evelyn looks untouched by violence. Death, so often ugly, appeared to have yielded to grace. Her ankles crossed, her hands folded, her face calm.

Strangers would project onto her whatever story they wished: doomed lover, tragic heroine, symbol of lost innocence. But behind the stillness was a storm of contradictions—a woman torn between duty and desire, between family expectation and self-preservation, between the longing to live and the certainty that she could not.

This book is not simply about the fall of Evelyn McHale. It is about the world that made her leap imaginable. It is about the silent pressures pressing upon women in 1947, the cultural fascination with beauty in death, and the haunting way a single image can echo through decades.

The camera shutter closed. The photo would travel further than Evelyn herself ever had, from New York sidewalks to glossy magazines, art galleries, and lecture halls. Yet beneath the myth, she remained a woman of flesh and doubt, not an icon but a daughter, a lover, a bookkeeper with ink-stained fingers. To understand Evelyn is to step back from the stillness of the photograph and listen for the voice hidden beneath it—the voice of a woman who could not reconcile her own reflection with the future laid before her.

And so we begin, not with the silence after the fall, but with the restless life that preceded it.

Chapter 1:

Roots in a Fractured Household

The first cries of Evelyn Francis McHale filled the walls of a modest home in Berkeley, California, on September 20, 1923. She arrived into a family already complicated by tension, one of seven children who would grow up beneath the long shadow of a mother's instability and a father's stern pragmatism. The McHales were not destitute, but neither were they free from the economic anxieties that haunted families across the United States in the interwar years. Her father, Vincent, worked as an officer in the U.S. Navy, a profession that demanded discipline and distance.

Her mother, Helen, struggled with depression and dissatisfaction that too often spilled into the lives of her children.

For Evelyn, childhood was not a steady landscape of innocence. Instead, it was a shifting terrain of upheavals and quiet crises. When she was six years old, her parents' marriage began to dissolve, their quarrels becoming louder, sharper, more public within the family home. The Great Depression had already unsettled millions of households, but for Evelyn it was not the stock market crash that defined instability—it was the disintegration of her parents' bond. By the time she reached adolescence, her mother had left the family, and the children were parceled out across relatives' homes, a scattering that fractured the continuity of family life.

This early rupture became a scar Evelyn carried inward, though she seldom displayed it outwardly. Observers remembered her as a quiet, reserved girl, never one to dominate a room, but always attentive to the currents of mood around her.

She learned, early, the survival strategy of silence—how to sense tension before it erupted, how to retreat into inward spaces where her own thoughts could not be intercepted.

Growing up in the 1930s meant coming of age in a country both weary of economic hardship and tentatively hopeful about renewal. Franklin Roosevelt's voice crackled through radios, promising a New Deal, promising security and possibility. Yet for children like Evelyn, whose sense of family had already fractured, the promises of government were abstractions. What mattered was the absence of her mother, the sharp memory of watching her leave, the whispered explanations from older siblings that never fully satisfied the ache of abandonment.

Evelyn grew tall and slender, with the kind of poise that suggested an inner reserve. Teachers described her as neat, diligent, and intelligent. Yet diligence could not erase loneliness. At school she was competent, even admired for her careful handwriting and her willingness to complete tasks without complaint, but she never seemed to carry the easy laughter of girls whose homes were intact. Instead, her friendships were polite rather than passionate, sustained more by circumstance than intimacy.

Her father, though dutiful, remained emotionally distant. Naval officers were trained to command ships, not households. He believed in structure, routine, and discipline, qualities he attempted to impose upon his children even as their family life cracked beneath the strain of separation. Evelyn's bond with him was complicated: she respected his authority, but she never felt the warmth of paternal tenderness. In moments of private reflection, she would later fear that she, too, had inherited her mother's fragility. She worried that beneath her surface of composure lay the same instability, a hidden flaw waiting to break through.

By the time Evelyn entered young adulthood, World War II had engulfed the globe. She watched her older brothers enlist, their uniforms symbols of both pride and absence. Newspapers were filled with stories of sacrifice and triumph, of Guadalcanal, Normandy, and Iwo Jima.

For Evelyn, the war years were defined less by heroics than by endurance. She found work in New York City as a bookkeeper, a role that demanded precision, order, and repetition—qualities she had cultivated in silence since childhood.

New York in the 1940s was a city of contrasts. Its skyline grew ever taller, its streets crowded with soldiers on leave, young women in skirts and victory rolls, businessmen racing toward postwar profit. The war brought new opportunities for women in the workforce, granting them wages and roles once reserved for men. Yet these opportunities came with expiration dates, for as soon as the war ended, cultural forces demanded that women return to domestic spaces. Evelyn stepped into adulthood at precisely this moment of contradiction: she could earn her own living and rent her own room, but the expectations of family and society whispered that her true destiny was to marry and manage a household.

It was in this context that she met Barry Rhodes, a young man from Pennsylvania studying to become an accountant.

Barry embodied steadiness. He was polite, attentive, and practical, with a future that seemed secure, a promise of financial stability and conventional happiness. Evelyn accepted his proposal not out of passionate abandon but from a quiet sense of inevitability. Marriage was what women did; it was the path from daughter to wife, from uncertainty to order. Yet even as she wore the engagement ring, doubts pressed against her mind like unwelcome intruders.

Those doubts were not visible to Barry, nor to her coworkers, who remembered her as gentle and composed. They were not easily spoken aloud, for in the late 1940s there was little vocabulary for the turbulence of depression, little patience for a woman's ambivalence about marriage. To hesitate was to seem ungrateful, or worse, unstable. And so Evelyn carried her anxieties inward, the silence of her childhood becoming the silence of her engagement.

But silence has weight. It accumulates. It gathers force until the pressure becomes unbearable.

Looking back, Evelyn's siblings would struggle to understand her decision in 1947. They would remember a young woman who smiled politely, who worked steadily, who seemed destined for the same ordinary contentment that filled the lives of millions of other young women across postwar America. Yet beneath that surface was the shadow of her mother's departure, the absence of maternal guidance, and the gnawing fear that marriage would trap her in the same cycles of disappointment.

In the photograph that would one day define her, Evelyn appeared serene. But serenity is not born from nothing. It is constructed, layer by layer, as defense against chaos. For Evelyn, that serenity began here, in childhood's fractures, in the disciplined silences of a girl who learned that to speak her fears was to invite rupture. Her calm face in death was the final mask of a life spent containing storms within.

Chapter 2:

New York at War, Evelyn at Work

The trains into New York were crowded with uniforms. Khaki and navy blue filled the stations, young men clutching duffel bags, young women clutching their hands in hurried goodbyes. By 1942 the war had transformed the city into a place of ceaseless movement—troop convoys on the Hudson, ration lines on street corners, factories working around the clock. For Evelyn, barely twenty years old, New York was not just a city of war. It was her chosen refuge, a place where she could step out from the fractured shadows of her childhood and claim the faint outline of independence.

She worked as a bookkeeper, one of thousands of women who had filled the clerical ranks during the war. The job was neither glamorous nor creative, but it offered something Evelyn valued: predictability. Numbers did not argue, ledgers did not leave. Where family had fractured and affection had wavered, the

She carried herself with a composure that masked the unease within, a composure so perfect that later, when she died, strangers would assume her serenity had been eternal rather than constructed.

It was in these years that Evelyn met Barry Rhodes, a man whose life seemed to offer the very stability she both craved and feared. Barry was studying to be an accountant, a profession as solid and dependable as the ledgers Evelyn filled each day. Their first meetings were unremarkable—casual, polite, marked by the tentative rhythms of two young people navigating postwar expectations. Yet Barry's attention settled on her, and in time, Evelyn found herself drawn into the orbit of his reliability.

Barry represented a promise: a future mapped out in clear, predictable lines. No sudden departures, no chaotic outbursts, no instability that would fracture the ground beneath her. For a time, Evelyn allowed herself to believe this was what she wanted. The world was rebuilding, and she could rebuild with it, anchored by a husband, a home, and a family.

When he proposed, she accepted. She did not shout with joy, but she smiled with the quiet composure everyone expected.

Still, doubts stirred in the recesses of her mind. The proposal came at a moment when women across the country were being asked to step back. The war was ending, soldiers were returning, and the message was clear: the independence women had tasted was temporary. They were to retreat from the factories, retreat from the boardrooms, retreat into kitchens and nurseries. Evelyn was not blind to this shift. She could see it in the newspapers, hear it in the conversations of her peers, sense it in the careful sighs of those who had grown to love their wages and feared their sudden loss.

For Evelyn, the engagement ring was not only a promise of stability—it was also a reminder of confinement. To marry meant to take on the role her mother had failed to embody, the role society still demanded. And Evelyn, haunted by the memory of her mother's unraveling, feared she would fail as well.

By 1945, New York had celebrated victory. Crowds filled Times Square, kissing strangers, waving flags, singing songs of relief and triumph. Evelyn stood among them, not in the frenzied center but at the margins, watching with a quiet smile that did not quite reach her eyes. The war had ended, but her inner conflict remained unresolved. The world's future was suddenly wide open, but hers felt narrower than ever.

She returned to her ledgers, her engagement, her routine. Outwardly, life proceeded in the neat columns of expectation. Inwardly, the silence gathered weight, pressing against her with every passing month.

Chapter 3:

Courtship and Quiet Doubts

The train from New York to Pennsylvania rattled through farmland and small towns, its windows framing a landscape that felt worlds away from the restless rhythm of Manhattan. Evelyn often traveled this line to visit Barry Rhodes, her fiancé, whose family lived in a modest house surrounded by the comfort of routine. Barry's world was one of careful balance sheets and predictable evenings, of conversations about community, hard work, and the simple joys of ordinary life.

For Evelyn, these visits were at once soothing and unsettling. She admired Barry's steadiness. His voice carried the confidence of a man who knew where he was headed. His plans were clear: he would complete his accounting studies, secure a position, and provide a dependable life for his wife. Evelyn recognized the security in this path, and part of her longed to surrender to it. She had spent too many years watching her own family fracture, too many years carrying the residue of instability. Here, in Barry's presence, the chaos seemed muted.

Barry's parents welcomed her warmly. They treated her as though she were already part of their household, folding her into dinners of roast meat and potatoes, evenings filled with polite laughter and the steady tick of the mantel clock. To them, Evelyn was an answer—graceful, respectable, a woman who would anchor their son's future. She smiled through the dinners, joined in conversations, and thanked them graciously, all the while carrying the quiet weight of expectation pressing against her chest.

The house smelled of familiarity: baking bread, polished wood, clean linens. To Barry's family, it was the scent of security. To Evelyn, it was sometimes a reminder of entrapment. She could almost hear the echoes of her mother's discontent in the background of these evenings, the memory of a woman who had walked away from precisely this kind of domestic promise. Evelyn had been a child then, too young to understand the complexities of her mother's despair, but old enough to feel the loss like an unfinished chord.

When Barry spoke of the future, Evelyn nodded. He spoke of a house they might one day own, of children who would carry their names, of routines that promised reliability. He was earnest, hopeful, certain. Evelyn answered with soft affirmations, unwilling to puncture his dreams with her doubts. To him, her silence was modesty. To her, it was survival.

Back in New York, the city's energy returned like a tide, and Evelyn felt briefly free again. The clatter of subways, the swell of office chatter, the anonymity of crowded streets—all of it gave her room to breathe.

Yet the ring on her finger was a constant reminder of a future narrowing into inevitability. She began to wonder whether she was capable of fulfilling the role expected of her. Could she become the wife Barry deserved? Or would she repeat her mother's patterns, unraveling beneath the weight of expectations too heavy to bear?

In her quiet moments, Evelyn rehearsed a script of reassurance. She told herself that doubt was normal, that all women hesitated before marriage, that once the ceremony passed, she would settle into the role. She tried to believe that her anxieties were shadows that would dissipate in the warmth of stability. But the shadows did not lift. Instead, they grew, expanding in the silence of her solitude, whispering questions she could not answer.

Sometimes she imagined her life with Barry as though it were already written in ledgers like the ones she balanced at work—columns of obligations, lines of routine, all neatly aligned. There would be dinners at six, accounts in order, children tucked into bed,

Sundays spent at church. It was not an unhappy picture, yet it left her restless. Something inside her resisted the script, as though to accept it would mean erasing herself entirely.

Barry did not see her unrest. He saw only her poise, her neat appearance, her polite smiles. To him, she was composed and graceful, the very image of a suitable wife. He could not know that beneath her calm exterior, Evelyn's mind turned over fears like stones in a pocket—worn smooth from constant handling, but never discarded.

The more Barry spoke of their marriage, the more Evelyn retreated inward. On the train rides back to New York, she would sit by the window, watching the Pennsylvania hills give way to the steel and stone of the city. With every mile, she felt herself suspended between two worlds—one promising security, the other offering anonymity. Neither felt entirely like freedom.

By the winter of 1946, her doubts had solidified into a kind of quiet certainty: she loved Barry, but she could not imagine becoming his wife.

The words never passed her lips, not to him, not to her coworkers, not to her family. Instead, they remained locked inside, waiting for the day when silence would no longer be enough.

Chapter 4:

The Weight of Expectation

By 1946, New York had settled into the uneasy calm of peacetime. The city still bore the scars of war—rationing signs fading from shop windows, veterans lingering in doorways with hollow eyes, factories shifting from weapons to consumer goods—but the air carried a new insistence: it was time to move forward. For women, especially, that forward movement had been carefully mapped out. Return to the home. Leave the factory floor. Step back into kitchens and nurseries, smiling, composed, grateful.

Magazines and advertisements reinforced the message with relentless cheer. Glossy spreads depicted young wives setting tables with perfect linens, mothers pulling pies from ovens, women radiant in aprons as though domestic labor itself were a form of glamour. Headlines promised happiness through conformity: "Be the Perfect Wife," "His Future Depends on You," "Your Place in the New America." To Evelyn, who already wore an engagement ring, the message was both affirmation and accusation. She was on the right path, yet she felt no joy in it.

At the office, her coworkers spoke easily of their plans. Some were newly married, others busied themselves with preparations, all seemed to accept their roles without hesitation. Evelyn listened, smiled, nodded at the right moments. But inside she felt like an imposter, as though she were walking through a life rehearsed for her by others. The numbers in her ledgers balanced neatly, but her thoughts never did.

Barry's visits to New York brought temporary relief. He would take her to dinner, walking with the quiet pride that she was his fiancée.

They laughed, they planned, they spoke of the house they might one day own. Evelyn tried to let his optimism wash over her, to silence the unease that coiled in her chest. But every plan seemed to carry a shadow. When he spoke of children, she remembered her mother's breakdowns. When he spoke of permanence, she remembered her mother's flight.

Her mother's absence haunted her more acutely now than it had in childhood. Back then, she had only understood loss as silence at the dinner table, an empty chair, unanswered questions. Now, as a woman on the threshold of marriage herself, Evelyn began to feel the echo of her mother's despair as if it were a premonition. What if she inherited the same instability? What if, no matter how hard she tried, she too would falter under the weight of domestic life?

She wrote little about her feelings, confiding in no one. Silence had become her defense, but it was also her prison. At night in her rented room, she would sit by the window, watching the glow of the city flicker against the sky. Somewhere in the distance, neon signs blinked promises of new beginnings, but for Evelyn, the future felt more like an inevitable narrowing.

The engagement itself grew heavier with time. Barry was steady, dependable, kind—yet his certainty pressed against her like a wall. He did not waver, so she felt she could not either. She told herself she was lucky to have him, lucky to be loved by a man with clear plans and loyal devotion. But the more she repeated it, the less she believed it.

In 1947, as the wedding drew closer, Evelyn's inner conflict hardened into something darker. She no longer saw her doubts as passing clouds. They became convictions: she could not marry him. She would fail him, fail herself, fail the image of the perfect postwar wife. The thought of walking down the aisle filled her not with anticipation but with dread.

Yet she spoke nothing of it. To her coworkers, she was composed. To Barry, she was affectionate. To the world, she was a young woman preparing for a secure future.

But inside, she felt as though she were standing on a narrowing ledge, the walls closing in, the air thinning. She had been balancing silence for so long that she no longer trusted her ability to speak at all.

The city's skyscrapers, once symbols of ambition, began to take on another meaning for her. She would look at them in passing—towers of glass and steel stretching toward the clouds—and feel the faintest tug of temptation. In their dizzying heights, there was a kind of promise: not of stability, not of conformity, but of release.

Chapter 5:

The Note Unwritten, Then Written

Spring settled over New York in April of 1947. Shop windows filled with pastel dresses and Easter bonnets, children tugged kites across Central Park, and couples strolled beneath budding trees. To an ordinary passerby, the city was alive with renewal. But to Evelyn, renewal felt like a demand she could not meet. Every advertisement, every wedding announcement, every smile exchanged between young mothers and children seemed to remind her of a role she was expected to step into—a role she already knew she could not play.

Her engagement ring still circled her finger, but she wore it with a sense of detachment, as though it belonged to another version of herself. When Barry came to visit, she smiled, kissed him, and listened to his steady voice as he mapped out their future together. He spoke of their wedding with enthusiasm, describing friends he wanted her to meet, the small apartment they might rent, the stability they would build. Evelyn answered in kind words, but her heart recoiled. She felt as though she were rehearsing lines for a play she had never agreed to perform.

It was during these weeks that Evelyn began composing, silently at first, the words that would become her farewell note. On her way to work she turned phrases over in her mind, testing them against her emotions. *He is much better off without me.* The thought had already become a refrain, not merely a sentence but a conviction. She saw Barry's future clearly: a dependable man, with a wife who matched his certainty, who carried none of her shadows. She imagined herself beside him and felt only the tightening grip of inevitability, a life not chosen but imposed.

Her coworkers noticed nothing unusual. She still arrived promptly, still balanced her ledgers with precision, still wore her clothes neatly pressed. If her voice was quieter, if her gaze sometimes lingered too long on the windows beyond the office, it was not remarkable enough to raise alarm. In 1947, depression was rarely spoken of openly, especially among young women who were expected to embody resilience. To falter was to fail, and Evelyn was determined not to fail publicly.

At night, in the privacy of her rented room, she sometimes wrote fragments on scraps of paper. Phrases about inadequacy, about her fear of becoming her mother, about her inability to be a wife to anyone. She tore most of them up, dropping them into the wastebasket before morning. Yet the words remained in her mind, sharpening into the shape of a final declaration.

By the last week of April, her decision had hardened into silence.

The photograph that would later define her death gives the illusion of serenity, and in truth, serenity had already begun to wrap around her like a shroud. She was no longer frantic, no longer restless. Instead, she moved with a calm certainty that unnerved only herself. There was relief in it—relief that the endless rehearsals of a future she feared would soon be over.

On April 30, she visited Barry in Pennsylvania one last time. They spent the day together quietly, walking, talking, holding hands. To Barry, nothing seemed amiss. She kissed him goodbye at the train station, promising to see him again soon. He believed her, because there was no reason not to. Her calmness convinced him, as it had convinced so many others, that all was well.

The next morning, May 1, Evelyn boarded a train back to New York. She carried with her the fragments of a note that she had now resolved to finish. Somewhere between Pennsylvania and Manhattan, the words crystallized:

"He is much better off without me. I wouldn't make a good wife for anybody."

The sentence was not dramatic. It was not the cry of someone desperate for attention. It was, instead, the voice of a woman who had already sealed herself off from the possibility of alternatives. For Evelyn, the note was less a plea than a final balancing of the ledger, an accounting of what she believed to be true.

When she stepped off the train in New York, the city bustled as always—vendors shouting on corners, taxis honking, businessmen rushing through crowded sidewalks. She walked through it with steady composure, carrying her silence like a veil. Within hours, she would transform from a face in the crowd into a name printed in newspapers, her story folded into the mythology of the city itself.

But on that last day of April, before the final climb to the 86th floor, Evelyn was simply a young woman with a note in her mind, a ring on her finger, and a decision that no one else could read.

Chapter 6:

Morning of May 1, 1947

The morning broke clear over Manhattan, the kind of crystalline spring day that sharpened the edges of every building. The Empire State Building gleamed in the sun, its limestone façade catching the light, its spire piercing the sky as if to remind the city of its ambition. Down on the streets, traffic surged, vendors shouted, schoolchildren tugged their mothers' hands. It was May 1, a day like any other.

For Evelyn McHale, it was the last day she intended to see.

She rose early in her small apartment, the same ritual as any workday. The bed was made neatly, the sheets tucked in with care. She dressed with precision: a gray skirt, white blouse, gloves, a jacket. Her engagement ring slipped back onto her finger. There was no outward sign of chaos, no hurried gesture, no mark of disorder. Composure had become her final mask.

On her dresser lay the note. Not long, not elaborate. Just a few sentences written in a steady hand:

"He is much better off without me. I wouldn't make a good wife for anybody. Tell my father, I too much of my mother's tendency."

It was the closest she had come to confession. She folded it carefully, placed it in an envelope, and set it where it would be found. No dramatics, only clarity. The words were the final balance of her life's ledger, as precise as any column of figures she had kept at the office.

She left her room and descended into the city's noise. The streets were alive with the energy of spring, and she moved among them unnoticed.

At Pennsylvania Station, she stepped off her train from Barry's town and onto the bustling platform. Commuters hurried around her, businessmen with newspapers tucked under their arms, women with shopping bags filled with fabric or bread. Evelyn moved with quiet purpose, her destination already chosen.

The Empire State Building was a monument to progress, built in the Depression as a symbol of resilience, now standing as the tallest building in the world. To tourists, it was wonder. To Evelyn, it was escape.

She entered the lobby, passed beneath the towering mural of the building itself, and approached the ticket booth. The attendant barely looked at her as he sold her the small stub for the 86th-floor observation deck. Another visitor among dozens, another face in the stream of strangers.

The elevator hummed as it carried her upward, the numbers glowing one by one, rising past offices, past midtown rooftops, until the doors opened onto the open air. The deck was crowded with tourists pointing cameras, couples leaning against the railing, children pressing their noses to the safety bars.

The wind was cool, tugging at coats and hair, carrying the scent of the city's smoke below.

Evelyn walked the perimeter slowly. She looked out over Manhattan—the East River shimmering in the sunlight, ships dotting the Hudson, rows of rooftops stretching endlessly north. For a moment she allowed herself to see what others saw: a city alive with promise, a world unfolding beneath her feet. But then her gaze settled inward again, toward the certainty she carried.

She leaned against the railing, composed as always. No one noticed her hesitation. No one asked her if she was all right. In 1947, strangers did not intrude, and Evelyn did not invite them. She waited for a space clear of others, a quiet corner where she could move without spectacle.

The calmness that had descended in recent weeks settled more deeply now. It was not the frantic despair of someone clinging to life. It was the quiet release of someone who had already let go. Her mother's shadow, her own doubts, her fear of failing Barry—they no longer pressed against her.

The silence inside her matched the silence she saw in the city spread below, tiny and far away, its sounds carried off by the wind.

She placed her gloves neatly on the railing, as if she were setting them aside for later use. She smoothed her skirt, tucked a strand of hair back into place. To any passerby, she looked like a woman simply adjusting herself before continuing her walk.

Then she climbed the railing.

The wind lifted her skirt slightly, the city rushed upward, and in an instant she was gone from the deck, a gray blur dropping toward the pavement below.

Tourists gasped, shouted, some reached too late. The elevator attendant heard the commotion but by then it was already over. Evelyn's fall was silent, a clean arc that ended in a single thunderclap of metal when her body struck the roof of a United Nations limousine parked on 34th Street.

On the deck, the crowd gathered, whispering. On the street below, people froze, staring upward at the building as if expecting to see the moment replayed. But all that remained was stillness, broken only by the voices of the first policemen forcing the crowd back.

Up in the sky, the spire of the Empire State Building still gleamed in the sun.

Chapter 7:

A City Holding Its Breath

The first sound was not a scream but the sound of metal giving way—an enormous, single-note rupture, like a church bell struck by lightning. It rolled down 34th Street and echoed off the limestone cliffs of midtown. Pedestrians looked around, startled, uncertain of where to place their fear. Then they saw the limousine: glossy black roof collapsed inward like a crushed tin, glass scattered in lucid glitter across the asphalt, and upon the caved-in metal a young woman resting as if a strange sleep had found her in the open air.

Someone cried out. Another person reached forward and then stopped, hands hovering, unsure whether to touch the figure whose calmness contradicted the violence that had delivered her there. A traffic officer, hat askew, blew his whistle as if order could be conjured by sound. "Back—back—give her air!" he shouted, a reflex more than a plan. Air could not help her now.

On the curb stood a boy with a paper sack of donuts, powdered sugar drifting from a split corner like low fog. His mouth was open. A secretary in a navy suit put a hand to her throat and said, "Oh," in a voice so small it might have been a prayer. Two men from the United Nations motor pool ran from the building, one slipping on safety glass and catching himself on the door handle that no longer had a window above it. They stared at the crushed roof as if looking hard enough could reverse the sequence of events.

A lean young man in a rumpled jacket stepped through the ring of uncertain bodies. He carried a camera like a musician carries a violin—tender, practiced, aware of the power locked inside a small machine.

His name was Robert Wiles, a student with an eye trained by habit more than experience. For a fractional moment he hesitated, human before he was photographer. Then the second habit, the one he had been feeding with hours in darkrooms and the weight of borrowed magazines, took him by the shoulders. He raised the camera.

The viewfinder cut the world down to edges and light. The chaos around him became a frame. He saw the limousine's buckled roof as a black sea and the woman upon it like a figure set afloat. Her right hand lay folded upon her left; her ankles crossed as if some private etiquette remained intact. A string of pearls—almost certainly glass, but luminous—rested against the pale column of her throat. Around her, shards winked in the sun. A corner of the Empire State Building's shadow grazed the car's fender, and beyond that shadow the street rippled with the startled choreography of onlookers.

Robert adjusted his focus. The city's noise dimmed in his skull. There is, for some, a pocket of quiet that forms in the middle of accident; he sank into it.

The light was clean, the shadows generous. He inhaled, metered by instinct, and pressed the shutter.

The sound—less a click than a crisp breath being taken—seemed indecently small in the presence of what had happened. He wound the film with a quick, careful stroke. Framing again, he stepped a little to the left, closing the composition around her hands, the collapsed metal, the stillness that felt less like death than like a story that had stepped outside of time.

"Hey—kid—no pictures!" a policeman barked, flustered, thrusting an open palm toward the lens as if it were a knife. But the command landed too late. The first frame already existed, a negative forming in the narrow darkness rolled tight inside the camera's belly. Whatever the city would say later, whatever names it would give the moment, the image had stepped into being.

Robert lowered the camera. His hands trembled in the complicated way that follows shock—a shiver that is part adrenaline, part shame, part reverence. He looked at the woman directly now, without the shield of glass.

Close up, the small abrasions on her cheek were visible; the slight bruise darkening along the collarbone; the meticulous neatness of her skirt, barely askew. He found himself searching, absurdly, for motion—a pulse at the throat, a flutter beneath the eyelid. There was none.

"Stand back!" another officer shouted, more force in his voice this time. A rope appeared from somewhere and was stretched clumsily between a hydrant and a lamppost. The circle widened. Curiosity pressed from outside it, grief and relief mixing into awe on the faces of strangers who had arrived too late to do anything but witness.

"Who is she?" someone asked.

A woman with red lipstick and a kitten-heel shoe missing its cap said, "She looks—peaceful," and then seemed ashamed to have uttered the word.

"From up there?" a man asked, pointing toward the spire, as if the building might answer him.

Inside the widening ring, a plainclothes detective knelt near the car.

He did not touch the body. He looked instead to the ground, reading the scattering of glass as if it were a language. The limousine driver, pale under his dark skin, stood off to the side. "I just parked," he kept saying, to no one particular. "I just parked."

Sirens drew closer at last, a thin wail that fattened into certainty. An ambulance nosed through the crowd with the patience of a ship easing into a tight harbor. The attendants jumped down with clinical efficiency, carrying a stretcher because that is the ritual, even when ritual is only a courtesy to the living. They shared a glance, wordless, acknowledging what any eye could see.

"Time?" one asked.

The other looked at his watch and said, "Eleven-oh-three," putting a nail into a timeline, as if the right measurement could anchor the day.

Robert stepped back, the camera suddenly heavy. He had the picture—perhaps he had several—but with the picture came a heat in his chest that was not triumph. He found a shadow of a doorway and leaned against the cool stone, watching how the city arranged itself around the event. Newsboys arrived, called by some street-born telegraph. A man with a fedora tried to argue his way under the rope and rebuffed, wrote furiously in a tiny notebook instead. In the office windows across the street, faces appeared as squares in a grid, mouths small and round, palms flattened to glass.

He thought—as photographers do when the shutter has already done its work—about exposure and focus and whether the tiny tremor in his hands had softened the frame. Then he thought about his mother, who would not understand why anyone would make a picture like this, and about his teacher, who would say that pictures were not made or unmade by permission; they lived or died by the truth of what they showed.

The attendants approached the limousine. One of them, older, with a mustache that seemed too careful for a man in so much hurry, paused at the car door as if approaching a chapel. He looked at her hands. "Folded," he murmured, not to anyone present but to the ledger of the day.

They worked gently. A blanket was produced, the bland gray of government supplies, and set aside for a moment—no need to cover yet, the detective indicated. Photographs would be taken by the department as well, measurements recorded, statements gathered. Procedure asserted itself, the civic immune system moving to close the wound.

Near the rope, two women spoke in undertones.

"Do you think she—was she alone up there?"

"They're always alone up there," the other said, and then bit her lip, hearing the cruelty in the generalization.

A breeze moved down the street, stirring the bright scraps of paper that always followed spring parades— flyers, sandwich wrappers, a theatre bill torn in two. One corner slid across the asphalt and came to rest against the heel of Evelyn's shoe. Robert saw it and, ridiculous impulse that it was, wanted to flick the paper away to keep the frame pure, keep the stillness unblemished. He did not move. The frame was already made; the world could be messy again.

The first reporter reached him with the speed of necessity. "You took pictures?" the man said, hat tipped, breath smelling faintly of cigarettes and urgency. "Kid, what's your name?" His pencil hovered, greedy and apologetic at once.

Robert said his name, surprised by the steadiness of his voice. He answered two more questions, then excused himself with the flimsy honesty of a student late for class. But his class today would be a darkroom; his teacher would be the chemical certainty of developer and fix. He had never carried a negative this carefully. He tucked the camera close, as if a crowd could bruise a photograph that had not yet seen light.

Before he left, he looked once more at the limousine. Perspective widened: the policeman now more composed, the motor-pool men quiet, the secretary still with her hand at her throat as if holding in a cry. Above them, the Empire State Building stood in its impassive glory. Tourists continued their slow revolution of the observation deck, peering between the bars, unaware that the ground beneath their feet had already spoken a sentence none of them would hear until tomorrow's papers.

He walked east, then south, then ducked through a doorway marked only by a bell and the faint smell of hypo. The darkroom greeted him like a confessor—red light, the tender clink of trays, the familiar arithmetic of time. He worked quickly, then not-quickly, fighting the urge to rush. Negatives hung like a row of thin glass ribs. He made a contact sheet, then chose the frame his hands had known in the moment: the limousine as altar, the woman as paradox, the city arranged around her like witnesses at an unplanned liturgy.

In the developer tray, the image rose by degrees— ghost, then rumor, then fact. Robert felt his throat tighten. The stillness on her face, the fold of her hands, the improbable cleanliness of the catastrophe: all of it surfaced from white into gray into the deeper tones where meaning lives. He slid the print into the stop bath, then the fixer, rocking the tray with a motion that had steadied him since he'd first learned the alchemy of light.

When he pinned the print to dry, he did not step back immediately. He stood close, as if proximity could teach him what the picture meant. He did not yet know the words the world would give it. He did not know that editors would dress the image in a phrase that pretended to soften it—*beautiful*—as if beauty could be a balm or an alibi. He knew only that the photograph was true—that it recorded not just an ending but a contradiction: the gentleness of her pose against the violence of her descent, the private decision made public in the most merciless way.

Outside, the day went on. The street was swept, the rope coiled, the limousine towed, the glass pushed into dull piles. The Empire State Building kept its appointments with tourists. In a rented room, a folded note awaited the hands that would find it. In Pennsylvania, a young man would soon be summoned to a phone he would not want to answer. In offices around the city, typewriters would clatter out the facts with a vigor that felt indecently fast.

And yet, for a little while longer, there was a thin pocket of quiet—a city holding its breath between event and explanation. Within that pocket, a student stood in a red-lit room, listening to the tiny sound a drying photograph makes as it tightens on the line, and understood—without yet finding words—that his life had just been braided to a stranger in a way neither had asked for.

He turned off the safelight. Darkness folded in with the soft authority of velvet. When he opened the door to the bright corridor, the print was ready to meet the world.

Chapter 8:

The Note and the News

The news traveled quickly, carried on the current of Manhattan gossip long before it reached the neat columns of the morning papers. By the afternoon of May 1, the Empire State Building had already resumed its routine, tourists buying tickets as if nothing had occurred, the elevators humming as though no one had stepped into the void. Yet on the ground, the echo lingered: a limousine under police guard, a detective's notebook filled with sketches and time stamps, and a folded piece of paper retrieved from a young woman's handbag.

The note was short, its handwriting steady, its tone devoid of drama.

"He is much better off without me. I wouldn't make a good wife for anybody. Tell my father, I too much of my mother's tendency."

For the detective assigned to the case, the words were simply evidence—an explanation, however incomplete. He copied them into the file, tagged the paper, and placed it in an envelope marked with the date. Suicide notes were not uncommon in a city that consumed dreams as readily as it produced them. Yet this one felt unsettling in its calmness. It did not plead. It did not accuse. It merely closed a ledger.

Barry Rhodes, in Pennsylvania, was summoned to a phone he would not have wished to answer. The voice on the other end was official, brisk, and merciless in its efficiency. His fiancée, they said, had taken her life. He listened, numb, his mind struggling to reconcile the news with the memory of the day before—her kiss at the station, her promise to see him soon, her hand warm in his.

She had given him no warning, no sign that their plans were anything but intact. He asked questions, but the answers were blunt and incomplete. A note, they said. A fall from the Empire State Building. Identification certain.

Barry hung up the receiver with a trembling hand. In the kitchen, his mother turned from the stove, reading his expression before he spoke. Silence stretched between them, heavy, until he managed the words: "It's Evelyn." His mother crossed the room, hands at his shoulders, but Barry shook his head, unable to bear the comfort. He left the house and walked without direction, carrying the impossibility of a future erased overnight.

In New York, reporters moved quickly. By evening, wire services carried the story: *Young Woman Leaps from Empire State Building, Dies on UN Car Below.* The bare facts were assembled into neat paragraphs—age twenty-three, bookkeeper, engaged to a Pennsylvania man, note found, police confirm death. The photograph had not yet circulated, but the story already carried the strange magnetism of spectacle. Suicide was tragic, but suicide from the tallest building in the world was something newspapers could not resist.

Robert Wiles's negative, drying in a student darkroom, was delivered to editors who knew instinctively what they held. The image was unlike any they had seen: a young woman, body intact, hands folded, face serene, resting as though sleep had taken her in the middle of the day. It would run in *Life* magazine within a week, accompanied by a caption that gave her no voice of her own—only the interpretation of others, who saw in her stillness an elegance she had never claimed.

At the precinct, Evelyn's belongings were logged: a handbag, a few coins, a lipstick tube, the note. Each item was entered in ink, recorded for the record. The officer writing the list did not pause to consider the life behind them. Procedure demanded only accuracy, not reflection.

Yet in the quiet of the evidence room, the note sat with its brief lines, holding within it the only words Evelyn had chosen to leave behind. They were not written for newspapers, not written for art, not written to become myth.

They were written for Barry, for her father, for herself—a final attempt at honesty after years of silence.

But already the city was transforming her. Already she was ceasing to be a daughter, a fiancée, a bookkeeper. Already she was becoming *the woman who jumped,* the figure on the limousine, the story told in elevators and on street corners. The private and the public had collided in the space of a single morning, and the collision had left Evelyn's humanity at risk of being replaced by legend.

In apartments across Manhattan, readers would glance at the next day's headlines and shake their heads. Some would pity her, some would condemn her, some would marvel at the drama of the act. Few would pause to imagine the years that had preceded the leap—the fractured childhood, the quiet doubts, the silence that had become too heavy to carry. For most, Evelyn McHale would be a name briefly encountered, then forgotten, except in the permanence of a photograph that would not allow forgetting.

Above 34th Street, the Empire State Building stood

untouched, indifferent, its spire still gleaming in the sunlight. It had seen thousands of visitors that day, thousands more would climb it tomorrow. But for one young woman, it had been an exit, and for the city, it had become a stage.

Chapter 9:

The Most Beautiful Suicide

The May 12, 1947 issue of *Life* magazine slid through mail slots and landed on kitchen tables across America. Its cover carried other headlines—politics, postwar optimism, the rituals of prosperity—but inside, tucked among pages of photographs and short reports, was an image that would outlive every other story in the issue.

On page twenty-three, readers found a full photograph: a young woman lying upon the roof of a smashed limousine, hands folded across her chest, face serene, skirt neat, pearls still at her throat.

The caption told them her name, her age, and the bare facts of her leap from the Empire State Building. The photograph itself told them something else entirely, though what it told depended on who was looking.

In kitchens from Maine to California, mothers paused with dish towels in their hands, staring. Some whispered, "How sad," before turning the page. Others lingered, unsettled by the contradiction: the violence of the fall erased by the tranquility of the image. To them she looked less like a victim than a bride who had lain down to rest.

Young men, flipping through *Life* while waiting for haircuts or bus rides, saw in her stillness a kind of glamour—tragedy packaged as elegance. College students clipped the image and pinned it to dormitory walls, half in fascination, half in rebellion against the banality of ordinary news. In art schools, professors held the photograph up to their classes, pointing to its composition, its surreal serenity, the way death had been framed as beauty.

The phrase surfaced quickly: *the most beautiful suicide*. It was not Evelyn's phrase. It did not belong to her, nor to Barry, nor to her family. It was a caption

manufactured by others, an aesthetic imposed upon her final act. The words traveled with the photograph, sticking like a label that could not be peeled away.

Barry Rhodes could not bear to look at the magazine. When he saw a copy on a neighbor's table, he turned it face down and excused himself from the room. To him, Evelyn's leap was not beautiful, not poetic, not symbolic. It was the shattering of a life they had planned together, the erasure of a future he had trusted. For days he replayed their last visit in his mind—her kiss, her promise, her calm smile. He had seen no warning, and the photograph only deepened his bewilderment. How could she look so peaceful, when the act itself had devastated him?

In New York, the photograph was discussed in offices and subway cars, in barber shops and cafes. Some condemned it as indecent, accusing *Life* of glamorizing tragedy.

Others defended it as art, insisting that beauty could be found even in despair. Few spoke of Evelyn herself. She had become an image, stripped of her contradictions, turned into a mirror for the culture's own obsessions.

Art critics compared the photograph to Renaissance paintings of martyrs, the calm repose of saints caught in moments of death. Sociologists debated whether the fascination revealed something dark in the American psyche. For many readers, however, the image required no interpretation. It was simply unforgettable.

In the offices of *Life*, editors congratulated themselves on publishing a photograph that would be talked about for weeks. They did not know it would be talked about for decades. They could not have predicted that artists, poets, and musicians would resurrect it again and again, each time peeling another layer from its original context.

Meanwhile, in a small evidence room, Evelyn's belongings remained boxed and labeled: gloves, handbag, lipstick, a few coins, and the note. The objects were quiet, ordinary, untouched by myth.

They belonged to a woman, not an image.

But the world was not looking at the note. The world was looking at the photograph.

In the years to come, strangers would remember her not as Evelyn McHale, daughter, fiancée, bookkeeper, but as "the most beautiful suicide." They would not know the weight of silence she had carried since childhood, the doubts she had hidden from Barry, the fear of becoming her mother. They would only know the serenity of her pose, the deceptive grace of a moment captured by chance.

The photograph had made her immortal, but not as herself.

Chapter 10:

Barry's Silence

The spring fields of Pennsylvania bloomed with a gentleness that mocked Barry Rhodes's grief. Apple blossoms dusted the trees in pale pink, the hills wore new grass, and the river near his parents' home shimmered in the morning sun. Yet Barry moved through it as though he were trapped in shadow. Days passed, but time did not seem to carry him forward. It circled back again and again to April 30—the day Evelyn had kissed him goodbye at the station, the day he had watched her board the train with the quiet certainty that they would see each other soon.

Now that kiss felt like a fracture, a moment split in two: before he knew and after he knew.

Neighbors came with condolences, their voices soft, their hands warm on his shoulder. They said the right words—*such a tragedy, so young, so beautiful, God's will*—but Barry could not accept any of them.

Each phrase sounded like paper attempting to cover stone. He thanked them mechanically, retreating as soon as he could. His grief did not want witnesses.

At night he lay awake, staring at the ceiling, Evelyn's voice echoing in his memory. She had not been dramatic, not melancholy, not unstable in the days leading to her death. She had been calm. She had promised him another visit. He replayed their conversations in obsessive detail, searching for signs he had missed—a pause too long, a glance too distant, a smile too forced. But nothing revealed itself. He was left with silence, and silence is the cruelest answer.

When the *Life* magazine issue arrived in town, Barry tried to avoid it. But he could not prevent its arrival in every barbershop, every waiting room, every friend's living room. The photograph was everywhere—on lips, in whispers, on the glossy paper that passed from hand to hand. His fiancée's body, folded neatly upon the crumpled roof of a limousine, was being called "beautiful." To Barry, the word felt obscene.

He forced himself to look once. The image struck him like a physical blow.

He recognized her pearls, her gloves, the curve of her cheek, the folded hands he had held countless times in his own. But she looked different—strangely serene, a version of her he did not know. The photograph had stolen her from him, reshaped her into something symbolic, something aesthetic. Evelyn the woman had been replaced by Evelyn the image.

Barry folded the magazine shut and did not open it again. He pushed it into the back of a drawer, but even hidden, the image lived in his mind. When he closed his eyes, he saw her as she had been in life—smiling at him across a table, brushing her hair back with a self-conscious gesture, walking beside him down a quiet

Pennsylvania road. Yet those memories now competed with the fixed stillness of the photograph. He feared, in time, the photograph would win.

The community tried to console him by suggesting reasons. "She must have been ill," some said. "She must have been overwhelmed." Others, less kind, whispered about weakness, about women who could not handle the pressures of life.

Barry said nothing. He could not explain Evelyn's choice, and he would not allow her to be reduced to gossip. He carried his silence like armor, though it only deepened his loneliness.

His mother worried. She tried to coax him into company, into chores, into conversation, but Barry resisted. He spent hours walking the fields, following familiar paths until they became blurred by repetition. Sometimes he carried a notebook, writing sentences that never quite formed into letters: *I should have known. I should have asked. I should have seen.* The words repeated until the page filled with nothing but guilt.

At night he dreamed of the train station—the moment of goodbye replayed in endless loops. In the dream he ran after her, called her name, pulled her back before she boarded. In the dream she smiled sadly and told him it was already too late. He woke from these dreams with his chest aching, his hands gripping the sheets as if he were holding onto her.

Weeks passed by. The world moved on. The photograph became a footnote in conversations about the Empire State Building, a curiosity passed among artists and journalists.

For Barry, it remained a wound that would not close. He no longer recognized the certainty he had once carried about the future. Accounting, marriage, children— those plans lay shattered, like the roof of the limousine that had received Evelyn's body.

In the quiet of his room, Barry whispered her name. It was all he had left that belonged only to him,

untouched by editors or captions or strangers' interpretations. He whispered it as prayer, as confession, as plea.

"Evelyn."

The word hung in the dark, unanswered.

Chapter 11:

A Photograph Becomes a Mirror

In the weeks following its publication, the photograph of Evelyn McHale began to slip free from the pages of *Life* magazine and circulate on its own. Torn from the magazine, pinned to bulletin boards, slipped into portfolios, discussed in lectures, it became something more than journalism. For some, it was art. For others, pathology. For many, it was a riddle they could not stop staring at.

In art schools across New York and Boston, professors carried the magazine into classrooms and held the image aloft.

They spoke of its composition—the diagonal line of the limousine roof, the contrast of crushed metal and tranquil face, the way the folds of Evelyn's skirt seemed untouched by gravity. Students leaned forward, transfixed, sensing that they were looking at something extraordinary, though not knowing whether to call it beautiful or grotesque. One instructor compared it to Caravaggio, another to the serene death

portraits of the nineteenth century.

Psychologists saw something different. In the quiet offices of Columbia and Yale, specialists in mental health debated what the note revealed and what the photograph concealed. Some argued that the calmness of her face was deceptive, a mask imposed by the lens. Others saw in her serenity a confirmation of their theories: that suicidal intent, once fully resolved, brought a strange relief, a quiet that could be mistaken for peace. Evelyn, they said, had reached that state of calm finality, and Wiles's camera had captured it for the world.

But in diners, barber shops, and corner groceries, the conversation was less clinical. Ordinary readers stared at the image and whispered about its uncanny power. A grocer in Queens taped it near the register, shaking his head every time he looked at it. "Looks like she's dreaming," he said to customers. A secretary on Long Island clipped it for her scrapbook, unable to explain why she kept returning to the page. A group of young veterans at a bar near Times Square argued over whether it was wrong for *Life* to publish it at all, one insisting that it glamorized despair, another saying it forced the country to look at what it preferred to ignore.

Evelyn herself was rarely mentioned beyond her name, her age, her role as fiancée. The details of her life mattered less to the public than the uncanny stillness of her death. She had been stripped of context, remade into symbol. Some saw her as a victim of postwar pressures, others as an enigma, still others as a tragic muse. But few asked about the fractured family she came from, the silence she carried, the doubts she had whispered only to herself.

Robert Wiles, the young photographer, found himself both praised and troubled. He was congratulated for having the instinct to raise his camera in that moment, yet he carried the unease of knowing his name would forever be tied to a stranger's death. His instructors urged him to build upon the fame the picture brought, to think of it as a portfolio piece. But Robert knew instinctively that he could never take another image like it. It had been a convergence of chance, tragedy, and instinct, and it weighed on him more heavily than any compliment could lighten.

Meanwhile, the term "the most beautiful suicide" began to attach itself to the image, passed from journalist to critic to casual observer. The phrase carried with it the unease of contradiction, turning Evelyn's final act into something consumable, almost aesthetic. Beauty, in this context, became a shield—an attempt to soften the violence of what had occurred. Yet for Barry Rhodes, and for those who had known her, the phrase was unbearable. There was nothing beautiful in the shattering of a life.

Still, the label stuck. The photograph had become a mirror in which the culture saw what it wanted: art, pathology, beauty, despair. Each interpretation said less about Evelyn than it did about the society gazing at her.

And so she lingered in the public imagination, a young woman transformed into myth, her private silence transmuted into a public story. The photograph traveled farther than Evelyn herself ever had, across oceans and into archives, into classrooms and galleries, into the minds of strangers who would never know her but would remember her face.

Chapter 12:

The Weight of 1947

America in 1947 was a nation suspended between triumph and unease. The war was over, victory secured, soldiers home, factories retooled for consumer goods. Department stores glittered with refrigerators and radios, suburban developments sprouted on farmland, and the newspapers spoke of a bright future powered by prosperity. Yet beneath the optimism lay contradictions that pressed upon ordinary lives like invisible hands.

For women, the contradictions were sharpest. During the war, they had stepped into shipyards and offices, flown aircraft, balanced ledgers, and supported a nation in crisis. They had tasted wages, independence, and responsibility. But peace had carried them back toward kitchens, urged by advertisements and government policy to relinquish their wartime gains. "Your husband needs you at home," read one campaign. "True fulfillment is family." Glossy magazine covers showed radiant wives in aprons, children clinging to their skirts, husbands arriving at the door with briefcases and smiles.

It was a vision of stability—yet it demanded a narrowing of self.

Evelyn McHale, bookkeeper and fiancée, found herself at the very edge of this cultural script. She embodied the qualities the era praised: modest, diligent, composed, ready to marry a dependable man. And yet the script felt to her like confinement. The memories of her mother's breakdown, the silent fractures of her childhood, sharpened the fear that marriage would not save her but trap her. The society around her offered no language for such doubts.

A woman uncertain about marriage was whispered about, pitied, or dismissed as unstable.

Psychologists of the day rarely helped. Popular theories cast women as naturally domestic, designed for nurturing roles, fulfilled only by motherhood and obedience. A woman who hesitated or resisted was often described in terms of "hysteria" or maladjustment. In that climate, Evelyn's fears could not be spoken without being misunderstood. Silence was safer, though silence brought its own danger.

The culture also glorified beauty in ways that blurred compassion with consumption. Postwar America was obsessed with appearances: the perfect home, the perfect wife, the perfect smile. Magazines taught women how to powder their faces, how to keep slim, how to ensure their husbands never strayed. Beauty was not simply admired; it was demanded, linked to worthiness itself. To be less than radiant was to risk failure as a woman.

It was within this framework that Evelyn's death—and the photograph of her body—resonated so deeply.

The image seemed to embody everything the culture prized: poise, beauty, composure. That she had died violently was secondary; what mattered, in the public imagination, was how serene she appeared. Her suicide was interpreted not as an act of despair but as a tableau of perfection. She had, in a grim way, fulfilled the script society had written for her: beautiful even in death, graceful even in tragedy.

But what the public did not see was the cost of those demands. Evelyn had not chosen to become an icon. She had chosen silence because silence was all that seemed available. She had chosen death because she believed no other option remained. In 1947, the culture had no place for women who did not fit the mold. It praised them for their beauty, their restraint, their composure—and then failed to notice when those very qualities concealed unbearable pain.

Historians would later describe the late 1940s as the beginning of a long repression, a decade when conformity was rewarded and deviation punished. The Cold War was beginning, and America prized stability above all.

But within that stability, many individuals—women especially—suffocated beneath the weight of expectation. Evelyn's leap from the Empire State Building was not only a private tragedy; it was also a symptom of a culture that left little room for voices like hers.

And so her death, once captured in a single photograph, became a mirror for the contradictions of her time. Postwar optimism could not erase personal despair. Beauty could not conceal instability. Silence could not protect against collapse.

What the photograph preserved was not only Evelyn's stillness but also the stillness of a society unwilling to look too closely at what lay beneath its polished surfaces.

Chapter 13:

The Photographer's Burden

Robert Wiles had never intended to be famous. He was nineteen, a student still fumbling with light meters and shutter speeds, practicing in borrowed darkrooms, dreaming of assignments he had yet to earn. When he raised his camera on May 1, it had been instinct, not ambition. And yet, in the weeks after the photograph appeared in *Life*, he found himself a name in conversations he was not present for, praised for a picture he could not quite claim.

Classmates congratulated him. "That shot—it's brilliant," one said, clapping him on the shoulder. Professors pointed to his work as an example of compositional instinct, urging other students to study the way his lens had transformed chaos into form.

Even strangers, hearing his name attached to the image, asked for his thoughts, his explanation, as though he had captured not only a picture but a truth.

But Robert felt no triumph. He carried instead a growing unease. The photograph had not been crafted. He had not arranged the light, positioned the subject, planned the moment. He had only been there, camera in hand, when tragedy unfolded. He wondered if pressing the shutter had been instinct—or intrusion. Had he honored Evelyn, or had he stolen from her the last privacy she possessed?

At night, in the red glow of the darkroom, he replayed the moment in his mind. The hush of the crowd, the folded hands, the small click of the shutter. He remembered how her face had looked without the lens—less serene, more fragile, with bruises forming beneath the skin. The photograph had smoothed those details, translated her into a symbol.

What he saw in memory and what the world saw in print were not the same.

Letters began to arrive at *Life*, some praising the image, others condemning it as indecent.

One minister called it "a glorification of sin." An artist in Chicago wrote to say it was "the most haunting photograph of the decade." Robert read these responses with a tightening chest. Each opinion seemed to build a wall around Evelyn, turning her into property of interpretation. None of them spoke of her as a person.

He avoided looking at the picture in public. When classmates pinned it to walls, he turned his head. When editors asked him to speak about his "artistic process," he muttered something vague about instinct. The truth felt impossible to say: that the moment had been raw, shocking, that he had pressed the shutter because it was the only thing he knew to do with his shaking hands.

The phrase "the most beautiful suicide" disturbed him most of all.

He heard it repeated in cafes, in classrooms, in whispers between journalists. It made Evelyn's leap sound like choreography, her despair like performance. Robert knew better. He had seen the twisted steel, the blood dark against the limousine's black paint, the stunned faces of the crowd.

There had been nothing beautiful in it—only stillness after violence. The beauty was not hers but the audience's projection.

Sometimes he considered destroying the negatives, erasing the image before it spread further. But he knew that even if he did, the copies already printed would live on. The photograph had left his hands the moment it entered the darkroom. It belonged now to history, and history rarely gives back what it takes.

He carried his camera differently after that day, not with the easy excitement of a student but with the caution of someone holding both instrument and weapon. When he raised it at later assignments—school protests, street parades, soldiers returning from overseas—he felt a hesitation, as though every frame asked him to justify itself.

Was he documenting, or was he consuming? Was he preserving truth, or bending it into spectacle?

Robert never stopped taking photographs. But he knew, even at nineteen, that no one would ever eclipse the one he had taken without meaning to. His career had been tied to a stranger's despair, and the knot would not come undone.

He did not know Evelyn McHale. He would never know her. Yet her face, serene upon a broken car, would haunt his work for the rest of his life.

Chapter 14:

Voices of Judgment and Fascination

By the summer of 1947, Evelyn McHale's name had traveled farther than she ever had in life. Not through personal acquaintances, but through columns, pulpits, and symposiums. Her photograph became a touchstone in debates about morality, psychology, and the uneasy direction of postwar America.

In churches across the country, ministers folded her death into sermons. Some warned of moral decay, arguing that Evelyn represented a generation losing its faith, seduced by modernity's emptiness. "She had everything," one pastor thundered in Ohio, "youth, beauty, promise—yet without God, it was not enough." Congregants nodded, reassured that despair could be explained by absence of devotion.

Other pastors spoke with more compassion, pointing to her silence as evidence of society's failure. "We must not only save souls," a minister in Boston said softly, "but also listen when the living cry out, even if they do so without words." Yet even these sympathetic voices used Evelyn less as a person than as a parable, her life reduced to a lesson for others.

Newspapers, eager for circulation, ran follow-up pieces. *The Daily News* published a spread comparing her photograph to Renaissance art, marveling at its "strange tranquility." A columnist in *The Chicago Tribune* condemned *Life* for sensationalism, insisting that beauty and tragedy should not be confused. Letters to the editor poured in: some praising the courage of publishing reality, others accusing the magazine of glorifying suicide.

A woman in Kansas wrote, *"I could not stop staring at her face. She looks as though she had simply decided to rest, and the world let her."* A veteran in Los Angeles replied, *"If you want to see beauty in death, look to the battlefield, not a girl who couldn't take life."* The photograph was no longer just an image; it had become a battleground of interpretation.

In lecture halls, the photograph appeared on projection screens alongside notes about depression, trauma, and "female maladjustment." Psychologists dissected her final words, parsing the phrase *"too much of my mother's tendency"* as evidence of hereditary instability. Some argued she had inherited depression; others claimed it reflected an unresolved Oedipal complex, fitting neatly into the Freudian frameworks still dominant in the era.

What none of them considered was the simplest truth: Evelyn's words were her own attempt to make sense of despair. But in academic journals, she became a case study rather than a person, her humanity dissolved into theory.

In diners, barbershops, and beauty parlors, Evelyn's story surfaced in conversations that drifted between

pity and fascination. "She was engaged, wasn't she?" one woman asked, shaking her head over a cup of coffee. "Imagine leaving a young man like that." Others spoke of her beauty with unsettling admiration, whispering that it was almost fitting that someone so graceful should leave the world in such a haunting image.

And yet, for every voice judging or theorizing, there were others unsettled into silence. People clipped the photograph and tucked it away in drawers, unable to explain why it haunted them. It was not just her stillness but the dissonance between the violent act and the serene image. The city had absorbed countless deaths, but Evelyn's was different: it had been captured at the precise intersection of horror and beauty, a paradox that refused to let go.

For Evelyn's siblings and her father, the attention was unbearable. They avoided the news, avoided the magazines, spoke of her only when necessary. The family had already fractured once in childhood; now it fractured again under the weight of publicity. To them, she was not a parable or a case study.

She was a daughter and a sister, lost. But the world did not want their grief. It wanted the photograph.

The voices multiplied, each claiming Evelyn for their own argument—moral, artistic, psychological. In the process, she disappeared further. The woman who had balanced ledgers in a Manhattan office, who had walked Pennsylvania fields with her fiancé, who had carried silence like a shield, became harder to see.

The photograph was clear. The woman inside it was fading.

Chapter 15:

A Family in Fragments

For the McHale family, Evelyn's death did not arrive as a headline or a photograph. It arrived as a telegram. The words were clipped, official, merciless: *"We regret to inform you..."*

Her father, Vincent, unfolded the paper at the kitchen table, his hands steady out of habit rather than calm. A Navy man by training, he had faced crises with composure, but this was different. He read the words again and again, unable to reconcile them with the memory of his daughter's soft voice, her careful politeness. He had known hardship—war, long deployments, the dissolution of his marriage—but the death of Evelyn was something for which no discipline could prepare him.

The younger siblings heard the news secondhand, whispered to them by relatives who did not know how to soften the truth. Some cried openly. Others stared in silence, too stunned to form tears. They had grown up in a fractured household already, scattered by their mother's instability and their father's sternness. Evelyn's death felt like another fracture, one that might never heal.

The note Evelyn left haunted Vincent most of all: *"Tell my father, I too much of my mother's tendency."* The sentence was both explanation and accusation, and he could not escape it. He wondered whether he had failed to shield his daughter from the shadows that had consumed her mother. He replayed the years of separation, the arguments, the silences. Had Evelyn absorbed her mother's despair in ways he had never noticed? Had his own distance deepened her loneliness?

He did not speak of these questions aloud. He carried them inside, allowing them to harden into regret. To neighbors who offered condolences, he nodded with the reserve of a military man, thanking them quietly, never allowing his voice to break. But at night, alone, he reread the note, his eyes tracing the words until they blurred.

For the siblings, grief took different shapes. One sister grew angry at the newspapers, furious that Evelyn's face had been spread across the country without consent. Another, younger, clipped the photograph and hid it in a drawer, ashamed of her fascination and horrified by her own inability to look away. A brother refused to discuss it at all, burying himself in work, muttering only that "the city swallowed her whole."

The family received letters—some from well-meaning strangers offering prayers, others from clergymen assuring them that Evelyn's soul could still find peace, a few from people who believed themselves experts, diagnosing her despair from afar. Each envelope felt like intrusion.

They stopped opening them after a while, leaving them in a stack that grew taller by the week.

The McHales did not attend public debates about Evelyn's death. They did not speak to journalists or contribute to the swelling discourse. They withdrew, protective of what little privacy remained.

To them, Evelyn was not "the most beautiful suicide." She was a daughter who had once helped with chores, a sister who had once shared secrets, a quiet presence whose absence now echoed louder than her voice had ever been.

Yet even in their retreat, they could not escape the knowledge that strangers now carried her image as their own. Evelyn's death had been folded into the city's mythology, into the nation's art and psychology, and the family could do nothing to reclaim her. She had been taken from them twice: once by her leap, and again by the photograph.

At the dinner table, when her name surfaced, silence usually followed. No one knew how to speak of her without unraveling.

Vincent sometimes cleared his throat and said only, "She was a good girl." The others nodded, each retreating into their own version of memory.

For the McHales, grief was not loud. It was not public. It was not beautiful. It was heavy, private, and enduring. And it would remain so long after the world forgot the headlines.

Chapter 16:

From Tragedy to Symbol

By autumn of 1947, the photograph of Evelyn McHale had already begun to escape the news cycle. Newspapers moved on to new scandals, new tragedies, new wars brewing overseas. But in art schools, galleries, and literary circles, the image refused to fade. It lingered like a ghost, a paradox too powerful to dismiss.

In Greenwich Village coffeehouses, young poets passed the magazine page from hand to hand, staring at the serenity of Evelyn's folded hands. Some saw in her a metaphor for the fragility of postwar optimism, others an emblem of rebellion against conformity. "She leapt," one aspiring writer murmured over a chipped cup of coffee, "because she could not breathe in the cage they built for her." The words were half-analysis, half-romanticization, but they stuck.

Painters tried to capture her. A student at the Art Students League sketched her form from the photograph, emphasizing the curve of her cheek, the contrast between her stillness and the wrecked steel beneath. Another experimented with abstraction, rendering only the folded hands and the pearl necklace, set against violent streaks of red and black. The instructors debated whether such exercises honored her or exploited her, but the work proliferated all the same.

Among intellectuals, Evelyn became a cipher. Essays appeared in small journals, musing on the photograph as commentary on modern alienation. One critic argued that her death represented "the collapse of the feminine under the weight of mechanized society," pointing to the smashed limousine as symbol of industrial modernity crushing the human spirit. Another described the image as "a twentieth-century Pietà," comparing her repose to depictions of the Virgin Mary cradling Christ.

For every interpretation, Evelyn receded further as a person. She became canvas, metaphor, symbol. Her own words—*"He is much better off without me"*—were overshadowed by words others imposed on her.

Not all artists glorified the image. Some recoiled. A sculptor in Brooklyn said flatly, "That photograph is theft. A woman's despair is not ours to frame." A photographer who had covered the war in Europe argued that it was dishonest: "She looks peaceful, but it lies. Death is never so kind." Yet even these protests only deepened the fascination, confirming that Evelyn's image demanded attention, demanded response.

In the years that followed, the photograph would resurface again and again. Andy Warhol would later screen-print her image in his *Suicide* series. Sylvia Plath, in her poetry, would allude obliquely to women who fell from great heights, serene in death.

Scholars decades later would return to the image as emblem of the era's contradictions. But even in 1947, the process had begun: Evelyn was no longer simply Evelyn. She was a story, a symbol, a canvas for others' unease.

Meanwhile, in quiet Pennsylvania, Barry Rhodes folded his memories tighter, unwilling to see her image displayed as art. And in California, Evelyn's siblings avoided galleries and magazines alike, unwilling to watch strangers dissect the sister they had known. For them, she was not a metaphor. She was family.

But the city—hungry for meaning, for beauty, for symbols—had claimed her. In the art that emerged, Evelyn lived again, though not as herself. She lived as an idea, and ideas cannot be reclaimed.

Chapter 17:

The Problem Without a Name

In 1947, no one yet spoke of "the problem that has no name." Betty Friedan would not publish *The Feminine Mystique* for another sixteen years. But the seeds of that restlessness—of lives confined to narrow roles, of ambition stifled by expectation—were already present. Evelyn McHale's death was not born in isolation. It grew in the soil of a culture that demanded beauty and silence from women, then puzzled at the despair such demands produced.

The war had unsettled traditional gender lines. Women had stepped into jobs once reserved for men, earning wages, managing responsibilities, discovering capabilities the culture had long denied them. But with the war's end came the retrenchment. Propaganda shifted: where once Rosie the Riveter flexed her arm, now advertisements showed apron-clad wives serving dinners to husbands who had returned victorious. The message was clear—women's wartime independence had been a loan, not a right.

For many, this retreat to domesticity was not unwelcome. Marriage rates soared, suburbs expanded, and the culture celebrated the promise of stability after years of global upheaval. But beneath the glossy advertisements lay a tension: women who had glimpsed independence found themselves pressured back into roles that felt suffocating. A quiet unease settled in households across America, though it had no language, no voice.

Evelyn lived at the cusp of this transition. As a bookkeeper in New York, she earned her own living, rented her own room, walked streets that allowed her to feel both invisible and free. Yet she was also engaged to Barry Rhodes, a man who represented security, tradition, and the future her culture demanded of her. For many women, this would have been a triumph: love, stability, purpose. For Evelyn, it was a narrowing corridor.

Her note revealed the fear at the core of her struggle: *"I wouldn't make a good wife for anybody."* The sentence carried with it the weight of a society that judged a woman's worth almost exclusively by her ability to marry and maintain a household. To believe she could not fulfill that role was to believe she had failed entirely. There was no alternative path offered, no model for a woman who chose differently.

The contradiction was unbearable: a culture that glorified women's composure yet dismissed their interior turmoil. To falter was to risk being called unstable, ungrateful, hysterical. Evelyn chose silence, and silence, over time, became its own kind of death.

Historians would later look back on the late 1940s as a decade of conformity. The Cold War amplified the pressure for unity, stability, sameness. Families were urged to be intact, marriages permanent, households orderly. Within that framework, women were praised for devotion and sacrifice, not for independence or voice. The "perfect wife" was both idolized and invisible.

Evelyn's leap from the Empire State Building, though deeply personal, resonated with these cultural contradictions. It was not only a young woman's despair—it was also a rupture in the story America was telling itself. A story of postwar happiness, prosperity, and domestic bliss. Her death was a reminder that beneath the polished surfaces, unease was growing, an unease that would not find full voice until the 1960s.

When the photograph circulated, people called it beautiful, haunting, tragic. Few called it inevitable. Yet in its stillness, the image exposed the cost of silence imposed on half the population. Evelyn's folded hands seemed peaceful, but what they concealed was the weight of a role she could not bear.

The culture did not yet have words for this contradiction. It would take another generation to name it, to challenge it, to write it into manifestos and books. But Evelyn's silence foreshadowed that future.

Her final act was not political by design, but it became political in resonance. She revealed, in a single leap, the invisible burden carried by countless women of her time.

Chapter 18:

The Long Shadow

Barry Rhodes sat at his desk, ledger open, pencil poised, numbers waiting. The columns blurred before his eyes. He had chosen accounting because it promised certainty: order could be achieved with neat sums, problems resolved by the balance of credits and debits. But in the weeks and months after Evelyn's death, numbers no longer offered comfort. He would add a column, check it twice, close the book, and still feel the unresolved deficit of her absence.

The town around him encouraged him to move forward. Friends invited him to gatherings.

Colleagues spoke of promotions and prospects. His parents urged him toward distraction, suggesting he take on more work, travel, even consider—eventually— meeting someone new. But Barry recoiled from the thought. The world spoke of "moving on" as if grief could be filed away like paperwork. For him, it clung like smoke, seeping into every room, every silence.

What made grief unbearable was not only the loss, but the public way in which it had unfolded. Evelyn had not died quietly in a hospital or by an accident in some remote place. She had leapt from the Empire State Building, and in leaping, she had been captured forever by a camera. Barry's fiancée was no longer his alone; she belonged to strangers who carried her image folded in magazines, pinned to walls, debated in coffeehouses.

When he walked the streets of Pennsylvania, he sometimes caught whispers. People had read the story, seen the photograph. They looked at him with a mixture of pity and curiosity. Some avoided him, unsure of what to say.

Others pressed their condolences upon him with the intrusive eagerness of those who wanted to taste tragedy secondhand. "She was so beautiful," one neighbor murmured, as though that were consolation. Barry forced a polite nod, but inside the words rang hollow. Beauty had not saved her.

At night, he returned to the moment of their last meeting. Evelyn at the station, her hand slipping from his, her smile calm. He had not known it was farewell. He had believed her when she said she would see him again. Now he replayed that scene endlessly, asking himself if he had failed her. Could he have asked more questions? Could he have seen beneath her composure? Could he have told her, in some stronger way, that she was enough? The questions circled endlessly, never resolving.

The note haunted him most. *"He is much better off without me. I wouldn't make a good wife for anybody."* When Barry read those words, he felt both sorrow and protest. He had never asked Evelyn to be perfect, never demanded that she live up to some ideal.

He wanted only her presence, her companionship, her hand in his. Yet she had believed otherwise, believed she would fail him. That belief wounded him more deeply than her absence.

In time, Barry attempted to return to normal routines. He resumed his studies, sat for examinations, accepted work at a small firm. On the surface, his life progressed as planned. But beneath the surface, Evelyn's shadow lingered. When he balanced accounts, he thought of the ledgers she had kept. When he walked through town, he remembered their strolls through Pennsylvania fields. When he saw the Empire State Building in photographs or film reels, his chest tightened, the skyline itself transformed into a gravestone.

The photograph followed him, unbidden. He avoided magazines, but it appeared in unexpected places: a clipped image on a colleague's desk, a reproduction in a psychology textbook, a reference in a conversation he overheard. Each time it surfaced, it was as if strangers had claimed a piece of Evelyn that did not belong to them.

To Barry, she was not "the most beautiful suicide." She was the woman who had laughed at his clumsy jokes, who had kissed him under the Pennsylvania sky, who had promised to share a life with him. The photograph stole that Evelyn from him, replacing her with a stranger he could not recognize.

In quiet moments, Barry wrote letters he never sent. Letters addressed to Evelyn, letters in which he told her the things he had not said. *You were enough. I loved you as you were. You would have made a wonderful wife.*

He folded these letters and tucked them into a drawer, knowing they could not reach her. But writing them gave him a brief illusion of connection, a way to speak into the silence.

Seasons turned. By winter, snow lay across the Pennsylvania fields, muffling the world into quiet. Barry walked alone through the drifts, breath rising in pale clouds, wondering if grief would ever release him. He knew the world expected him to remarry one day, to build the life Evelyn had abandoned. Perhaps he would. But he also knew that no matter what future unfolded, a part of him would remain in 1947, standing on the platform as Evelyn boarded the train, watching her disappear into the city that would take her from him.

In that sense, Barry understood something the newspapers and artists never did: Evelyn's death was not beautiful, not symbolic, not art. It was a wound, raw and private, carried not by the culture but by those who had loved her. For him, she would never be an icon. She would always be the woman whose absence weighed heavier than her presence ever had.

Chapter 19:

The City and the Void

In the months after Evelyn's death, New York carried on with its relentless rhythm. The sidewalks filled with shoppers, the subways groaned with commuters, and the skyline glittered in the spring sun. To most, the Empire State Building remained what it had always been: a symbol of American ambition, the pinnacle of modern engineering. But for some, the knowledge that a young woman had leapt from its heights lodged like a splinter in the imagination.

Writers in small magazines began to use her story as shorthand for the city's contradictions. "She did not leap into despair alone," one essayist claimed, "she leapt from the altar of modernity itself."

The Empire State Building was not merely a tall structure; it was a monument to progress, to capital, to the very forces that both promised fulfillment and delivered alienation. Evelyn's body landing on the roof of a limousine—a vehicle for diplomats of the United Nations, no less—seemed to critics a bitter metaphor for the gap between personal despair and global triumph.

Sociologists debated whether suicide was becoming a modern epidemic. They quoted Émile Durkheim's theories of anomie, pointing to Evelyn as an example of how industrial society severed individuals from meaningful community. They saw her death not as a private act but as a symptom of the alienation produced by cities where millions lived together in anonymity, unseen even as they brushed shoulders on crowded sidewalks.

Journalists, too, leaned on the theme of urban despair. A columnist in *The New Yorker* wrote that Evelyn's leap was "the dark side of the skyline," proof that the very towers designed to inspire could also invite escape.

Letters poured in, some condemning the writer for romanticizing tragedy, others confessing that they too had felt dwarfed by the city's vastness.

In coffeehouses and student dormitories, young people spoke of Evelyn in tones that mixed awe and unease. For them, she was not only a woman who could not bear marriage but a symbol of how the city swallowed individuality. "You can live here your whole life and still disappear," one student remarked, staring at the photograph clipped from *Life*. Evelyn had disappeared not through neglect, but through an act that forced the city to see her, if only for a moment.

The discourse unsettled city officials. The Empire State Building's management quietly increased patrols on the observation deck, adding guards, adjusting railings, instructing staff to watch for hesitation. They wanted no more headlines, no more photographs. Yet they knew they could not erase what had already happened. The building's majesty now carried a shadow. Tourists still marveled at the view, but some, stepping to the edge, shivered at the thought of the woman who had leapt.

Even beyond New York, the story rippled into discussions of postwar life. America was prosperous, victorious, on the cusp of suburban expansion and consumer plenty. But Evelyn's leap suggested that prosperity was not enough. Beneath the surface optimism lay cracks: women uneasy with domestic roles, veterans struggling with memories of battle, workers worn down by repetition and anonymity. Suicide rates did not spike dramatically, but the cultural fear was palpable: what if modern life itself was the weight pressing people toward despair?

Evelyn's note—*"I wouldn't make a good wife for anybody"*—was rarely quoted in these debates. It was too personal, too particular. Instead, the photograph was used as shorthand, a visual metaphor stripped of context. The woman became less important than the image, the image less important than the meanings imposed upon it. To those debating urban alienation, Evelyn was not Evelyn. She was evidence, a symbol, a shadow cast by a skyscraper.

But beneath the intellectual debates, ordinary citizens felt something simpler: unease.

They clipped the image and kept it not because they saw philosophy in it, but because it disturbed them. It forced them to acknowledge a truth they preferred to ignore that beneath the polished surfaces of postwar prosperity, despair lived quietly, sometimes invisibly, until it could no longer be contained.

For New York, Evelyn's leap was not the first suicide, nor would it be the last. But it was the one that lodged in memory, crystallized by a photograph that would not allow forgetting. The city continued to rise, to build, to proclaim itself the pinnacle of modern life. Yet within its towering heights, Evelyn had revealed the abyss.

Chapter 20:

Across the Atlantic

In 1947, Europe was still rubble and scaffolding, a continent patching its wounds from six years of war. London carried the smoke stains of the Blitz; Paris still whispered with the memory of occupation; Berlin was a scar divided by rubble and hunger. Amid ration books and reconstruction, Evelyn McHale's image crossed the ocean tucked inside *Life* magazine, carried in the satchels of American diplomats, the hands of soldiers, the crates of exports.

In Paris, the photograph found an audience attuned to tragedy.

French intellectuals, steeped in existentialism, recognized in Evelyn's stillness a paradox they had already been articulating: the absurdity of existence, the inevitability of death, the confrontation with nothingness. At the Café de Flore, young philosophers argued over the image, sipping bitter coffee under a haze of Gauloises smoke.

Jean-Paul Sartre, though never writing directly of Evelyn, would have seen in her leap the absurd: a refusal of a prescribed role, a confrontation with freedom so unbearable it collapsed into finality. Simone de Beauvoir, had she glimpsed the photograph, might have seen in Evelyn's note the crushing weight of gender expectation—*"I wouldn't make a good wife for anybody"*—the clearest evidence of a world that measured women only by their capacity to marry and serve.

In London, the photograph circulated among artists and journalists who compared it to the stoicism of wartime civilians. "She lies as if she had endured the Blitz itself," one critic wrote, "unbroken even in death."

The remark said more about Britain's need to see resilience than about Evelyn herself. Yet the image resonated: here was a young woman whose stillness seemed to carry dignity even in despair.

Across the continent, in cities where ruins still dominated skylines, Evelyn's photograph was received less as sensationalism and more as symbol. To Europeans, death was not an abstract tragedy—it was a neighbor, a companion, a shadow that still stretched across streets lined with craters. But Evelyn's death was different. It was not inflicted by bomb or bullet. It was chosen. That choice unsettled them.

In galleries from Paris to Amsterdam, reproductions of the image began to appear. Some were pinned discreetly to classroom boards, others slipped into collages alongside war photographs. Artists debated whether Evelyn's leap was a uniquely American story— the despair hidden beneath prosperity—or whether it echoed universal truths about alienation in the modern age.

In Germany, where rubble still defined daily life, the image circulated more slowly. But when it did appear, critics noted the strange contrast: while Europeans had endured suffering imposed upon them, Evelyn had carried despair from within. To them, it was an alien tragedy—yet also a reminder that the human psyche, even in peace, could collapse.

What united the international reception was fascination. Evelyn's leap, frozen in Robert Wiles's photograph, was more than news. It was a visual riddle that crossed languages and borders. Each culture saw itself reflected in her stillness: France saw existential dread, Britain saw stoic composure, Germany saw the fragility of the mind after destruction.

Yet in each retelling, Evelyn disappeared further. She was not remembered as a bookkeeper, as Barry's fiancée, as Vincent's daughter. She was an idea, reshaped again and again to suit the anxieties of others.

By the early 1950s, the photograph had become part of an international dialogue on despair and beauty, quoted in art journals, referenced in lectures, invoked in conversations about modernity itself.

The young woman who had felt invisible in life had become inescapable in death.

And yet, for all the distance her image traveled, the silence of her voice remained. She had left only a note, brief and plain. Everything else was projection.

Chapter 21:

America's Anxious Mirror

By 1949, the photograph of Evelyn McHale was no longer just a curiosity pinned to classroom walls or reprinted in small art journals. It had become, for many outside the United States, a symbol of something larger: the tension between America's glittering surface and the shadows beneath. As the Cold War hardened lines between East and West, Evelyn's leap from the Empire State Building was reinterpreted not merely as a personal tragedy, but as a metaphor for a superpower's unease.

In Paris, essays appeared in leftist journals arguing that the photograph revealed "the sickness of capitalist society." America boasted skyscrapers, prosperity, and consumer abundance, but here was a young woman crushed against a limousine—wealth and despair fused into a single tableau. To critics already skeptical of American triumphalism, Evelyn's death was evidence that beneath the shine of Coca-Cola and jazz records lay alienation and emptiness.

In Moscow, propagandists seized on the image. Soviet newspapers reproduced the photograph alongside headlines about exploitation and decadence. "This is the reality of American women," one article proclaimed, "discarded by a system that values them only as decoration." Of course, the Soviet Union had its own hidden tragedies, but Evelyn's serene face against twisted steel became useful in the ideological contest. She was transformed into proof that the capitalist dream devoured its own children.

Even in Western Europe, where American aid was rebuilding cities through the Marshall Plan, Evelyn's photograph unsettled faith in the promised new order. Intellectuals saw her death not as an isolated act but as the embodiment of contradictions: the tallest building in the world sheltering despair, progress failing to shield an individual from collapse. "A skyscraper is not a home," one London critic wrote. "It is a monument. And monuments are cold."

Meanwhile, in America, the image was still being quietly discussed in classrooms and coffeehouses, though fewer newspapers mentioned her name. The public had shifted to other stories, other tragedies. But abroad, Evelyn was being reimagined as emblem. She was no longer Evelyn McHale, a 23-year-old bookkeeper. She was "the girl who leapt from America's tower," her body stretched across debates about ideology, morality, and modernity.

Barry, in Pennsylvania, never read the Soviet papers or the Parisian essays. But had he seen them, he would have recoiled. To him, Evelyn was not a symbol of capitalism's failure or modernity's alienation. She was a woman he had loved, whose absence still cut him open each night. The gulf between public myth and private grief widened with each retelling.

Back in New York, the Empire State Building remained untouched, its observation deck drawing thousands. Tourists gazed outward toward the Atlantic, where ships carried goods and ideas in both directions. Few of them thought of Evelyn as they leaned against the railings. Her death had been absorbed into a broader narrative, one that no longer needed her details to make its point.

What the Cold War made of Evelyn was projection. She was a mirror onto which nations cast their anxieties: America's prosperity as shallow, its women as trapped, its skyscrapers as symbols of grandeur without warmth. Her leap became commentary, not confession. And yet, in that commentary, her own voice was lost once again.

By the end of the 1940s, Evelyn existed in two parallel forms. In Barry's heart, in her family's grief, she was a daughter and fiancée, remembered in private silence. In the international press, she was a metaphor, folded into ideological battles, cited as evidence in debates she had never chosen.

The photograph had crossed oceans, but Evelyn herself had vanished beneath the weight of meaning others imposed upon her.

Chapter 22:

Beauty in Death

By the early 1950s, Evelyn McHale's photograph had shifted from news into something more enduring: an artifact of culture. It surfaced in art classes, philosophy seminars, and hushed conversations among writers who were increasingly drawn to the paradox of beauty entwined with tragedy. For a nation that prided itself on vitality and progress, there was a peculiar allure in contemplating a death that appeared, at least in the image, so serene.

In New York literary circles, her name resurfaced in essays about the nature of modern beauty.

Small magazines ran meditations comparing her image to Keats's notion that beauty and truth were bound together. Poets, still wrestling with the legacy of war, saw in her stillness a metaphor for the fragility of peace. One young poet wrote: *"She lies not as a casualty of battle, but of the quiet war within. And in her folded hands the city sees itself reflected."*

The essayists rarely quoted her note; it was too stark, too ordinary. Instead, they lingered on her face, her pose, her strange repose amid twisted steel. They romanticized what Evelyn herself had never claimed, turning her despair into a symbol of purity, even of transcendence.

In downtown galleries, photographs of ruins from Europe hung beside new works from American painters. Among them, clipped reproductions of Evelyn's photograph sometimes appeared, offered not as journalism but as art. Abstract painters studied the contrast between the smooth curve of her body and the jagged lines of the wreckage beneath. Some even repainted the image in oils, altering colors, softening shadows, heightening contrast—transforming her into something stylized, distant from the violence that had delivered her there.

Not all viewers approved. Critics asked whether such use of the image commodified despair. Yet audiences came, drawn less by the debates than by the unsettling calmness of the figure on the limousine roof. For them, the photograph had become a meditation piece: a modern memento mori, reminding them that death could intrude even in a world devoted to progress.

Ordinary readers, too, found themselves unable to forget the image. In barbershops and corner stores, the clipped page still lingered years later, yellowing at the edges. Customers would glance at it and shake their heads, repeating the phrase that had become attached to her: *the most beautiful suicide*. It was not admiration so much as bewilderment—an attempt to explain the unexplainable by clothing it in beauty.

In private homes, some kept the photograph tucked in scrapbooks or diaries. These were not collectors of morbidity but people who sensed in Evelyn's stillness a truth they could not name.

The photograph was unsettling, but it was also magnetic. It invited contemplation in a way ordinary news did not.

Psychologists, too, returned to the image, puzzled by the serenity of her face. They spoke of the "paradox of composure," suggesting that those most resolved to die often appeared most calm. For them, Evelyn's photograph was evidence of a theory: that the decision itself brought relief, smoothing the turmoil that had preceded it. In seminars, the image appeared on slides, students taking notes as though the young woman on the limousine were a case study, not a life.

Yet these discussions rarely touched the deeper truth: Evelyn had not died for theory or art. She had died because silence had pressed too heavily, because her fears of inadequacy had left her no room to breathe.

What united these varied appropriations—writers, artists, psychologists, the public—was the transformation of Evelyn into symbol. She became less of herself and more a vessel for the era's anxieties and obsessions. In a time when America celebrated vitality, consumerism, and the family ideal,

Evelyn's serene death offered a dark counterpoint: beauty preserved not in life but in surrender.

For Barry Rhodes, for her siblings, this appropriation was unbearable. They did not read the essays or attend the galleries, but they heard whispers, saw clippings, caught glimpses. To them, the fascination was a theft. Evelyn had not leapt to become an icon. She had leapt because she saw no other way forward.

But culture has a way of reshaping individuals into metaphors, and by the 1950s, Evelyn was no longer remembered primarily as a daughter, a sister, a fiancée. She was remembered as an image—folded hands, serene face, pearls against pale skin. She had been claimed by the strange American tradition of finding beauty in tragedy, of polishing despair into art.

And so she endured, not in the memories of those who had known her best, but in the imagination of strangers who could not look away.

Chapter 23:

Conformity and the Cold War Mind

The 1950s arrived draped in optimism. The GI Bill opened doors to college and home ownership. Suburbs sprawled outward from cities like rings on a tree, each house a promise of security, each lawn manicured into proof of stability. Magazines celebrated radiant families gathered around televisions, wives in pearls, husbands with briefcases, children in pressed clothes. To the world, America was thriving, the embodiment of victory and prosperity.

Yet beneath the surface, unease crept like a shadow at the edge of the picture. The Cold War intensified, sirens drilled schoolchildren to duck beneath desks, and whispers of nuclear annihilation haunted even quiet neighborhoods. The House Un-American Activities Committee staged hearings, demanding conformity not only in action but in thought. Suburban sameness was not simply a lifestyle — it was a defense, a bulwark against suspicion.

In this landscape, Evelyn McHale's death acquired a new resonance. Though few still spoke her name, the photograph lingered, haunting certain conversations about the cost of conformity. To some cultural critics, she was an early warning: a young woman who could not bear the narrow role prescribed to her. Her leap from the Empire State Building became, in hindsight, a fracture line across the gleaming surface of postwar stability.

Nowhere were the pressures sharper than for women. The war had given them independence — wages, skills, purpose — only for peace to confine them again to kitchens and nurseries. Advertisements proclaimed that fulfillment lay in a sparkling home and a satisfied husband, but many women felt a gnawing dissatisfaction they could not name.

Betty Friedan would later call it "the problem that has no name," but in the 1950s, it was simply silence.

Evelyn's note — *"I wouldn't make a good wife for anybody"* — became, for some scholars looking back, a prophecy of that silent unrest. She was not rebelling against Barry alone, but against a system that measured her entirely by her potential as a wife. In the context of the 1950s, her words read like an indictment of the roles that so many women felt suffocated by but could not challenge aloud.

Psychologists noted a troubling trend: while the nation grew richer, suicide rates did not fall. Wealth and conformity did not guarantee contentment. Cases like Evelyn's hovered in the background as silent commentary. If prosperity and stability were the cure for despair, why did despair persist?

Some commentators saw her leap as symbolic of the loneliness bred by modern urban life. Others argued it reflected the hollowness of suburban promises, where individuality was sacrificed to sameness. The Empire State Building — icon of American ambition — became, in her story, both monument and escape route.

Abroad, Evelyn's image had been used as propaganda. At home, the Cold War lens colored her story differently. Intellectuals whispered that her death revealed the fragility of the American psyche, a vulnerability the Soviets might exploit. The fear was not only of bombs and spies, but of internal weakness: that beneath the confident surface, America's citizens carried doubts, restlessness, despair. Evelyn, serene in death, became one of many reminders that the Cold War was fought not only in geopolitics but in the human soul.

In living rooms across the country, Evelyn's name was rarely spoken. Families preferred the narrative of progress, of victory, of harmony. Tragedy was tucked away, silence preserved appearances. In this sense, Evelyn's story mirrored countless others. Her leap had been spectacular, unforgettable because it was photographed. But many other women, many other men, carried despair quietly, hidden in kitchens and offices, never photographed, never published.

The 1950s prided itself on conformity, but Evelyn's death lingered as an unspoken reminder of the cost. She was not remembered by most as a rebel, nor as a prophet. She was remembered as an image — folded hands, serene face — but the resonance of that image deepened as America's culture of silence pressed harder.

Her leap was not simply into the void of 34th Street. It was into the void of a society unable, or unwilling, to give language to the struggles within.

Chapter 24:

Toward Immortality in Art

By the end of the 1950s, the photograph of Evelyn McHale had taken on a second life, divorced almost entirely from the circumstances of her death. It appeared in anthologies of photography, pinned to bulletin boards in universities, and whispered about in literary salons. For many young writers and artists, the image was no longer journalism but a kind of modern myth — a reminder that beauty and death could collide in a single frozen instant.

In small poetry journals, her image reappeared as metaphor.

Writer's spoke of women who "fell from towers" and "slept on steel," invoking Evelyn without naming her. The calmness of her repose became a recurring symbol — not of despair, but of surrender wrapped in elegance. Some poets romanticized her, casting her as a tragic bride who refused the altar. Others, more cynical, saw her as a warning against the suffocating scripts of domesticity.

In these verses, her note — *"I wouldn't make a good wife for anybody"* — was sometimes echoed in lines about silence, expectation, and the invisible weight of marriage. What Evelyn had meant as plain confession was reshaped into lyrical prophecy.

Novelists, too, borrowed from her. In the late 1950s, short stories appeared in literary magazines featuring women who stood at windows, gazing down at the city with quiet desperation. One novel, never widely read but striking in hindsight, opened with a scene unmistakably modeled on Evelyn: a young woman descending a New York skyscraper not by elevator, but by choice.

The character's motives differed, but the inspiration was clear.

Writers rarely named her, but the photograph was always there — clipped, pinned, remembered. Evelyn had become raw material; her life and death stripped for narrative use.

By the early 1960s, the photograph had entered the orbit of Andy Warhol. Fascinated by the interplay of death and celebrity, Warhol collected clippings of accidents, suicides, and disasters. Among them was Evelyn. In his *Suicide* series, he screen-printed her image in stark repetition, stripping away context until she was pure form, pure symbol.

Warhol's treatment disturbed many, but it also cemented Evelyn's place in art history. She was no longer simply the subject of a student's accidental photograph; she was part of the Pop Art commentary on mass media, tragedy, and beauty. Multiplying her image across canvases, Warhol turned Evelyn into what the culture had already made her: consumable.

For critics, Warhol's use of her image raised unsettling questions. Was this exploitation or exposure? Was he trivializing her despair, or forcing viewers to confront their own voyeurism? The debates swirled, but the image endured. Each reproduction pushed Evelyn further from herself, but closer to immortality.

College students in the 1960s, drawn to rebellion and disillusionment, rediscovered the photograph. Some saw in her leap an act of protest against conformity. Others viewed her as a symbol of fragility in an age of upheaval. The photograph circulated in dorm rooms alongside posters of Che Guevara and Bob Dylan, unlikely companions in the pantheon of icons.

For young women, the fascination was more complicated. Some whispered that Evelyn had chosen the only way out of the suffocating roles their mothers still inhabited. Others recoiled at the romanticization, insisting that despair should not be mistaken for liberation. Yet even in disagreement, her presence lingered.

By the 1960s, Evelyn McHale had become something she had never sought: immortal.

Not in the way of saints or politicians, but in the way of symbols — endlessly reinterpreted, endlessly projected upon. Her leap from the Empire State Building had ended one life, but it had birthed countless retellings, each less about her than about the culture gazing at her.

For Barry Rhodes, for her siblings, this immortality was unbearable. They had wanted Evelyn to rest. Instead, the world kept resurrecting her — not as daughter, not as fiancée, not as sister, but as an image, folded and unfolded, again and again.

Chapter 25:

Echoes in the Age of Upheaval

The 1960s arrived like a rupture. Civil rights marches filled the streets, students occupied campuses, music thundered from radios with new defiance. America's polished façade of the 1950s cracked, revealing long-suppressed discontent. Women, in particular, began to question the roles they had been assigned, the silences they had been forced to inhabit. Into this climate, the image of Evelyn McHale reemerged with fresh resonance.

By the mid-1960s, Betty Friedan's *The Feminine Mystique* had given language to what Evelyn's note had foreshadowed: the despair of women confined to roles as wives and mothers, denied expression beyond domestic walls. Feminists looked back at Evelyn's words — *"I wouldn't make a good wife for anybody"* — and saw in them the quiet scream of a generation. She had not lived to see the women's movement, but her silence became, in retrospect, a kind of prelude.

Articles in feminist journals pointed to her death as evidence of the "invisible cost" of enforced domesticity. "She leapt not from a building," one writer argued, "but from a script that offered her no place to breathe." Others cautioned against romanticizing her act, insisting instead on seeing it as indictment: a life cut short by cultural constraints, not by personal weakness.

At the same time, existentialist thought, imported from Paris and embraced by American students, seized on Evelyn's image as emblem of "the absurd." To some, her leap represented the confrontation with freedom Sartre and Camus had described: when life's meaninglessness became unbearable, the individual confronted the void.

Photographs of Evelyn appeared in philosophy seminars alongside passages from *The Myth of Sisyphus*.

For those steeped in existentialism, her stillness after the fall was not beauty but defiance: an individual who, faced with a script she could not inhabit, chose exit on her own terms. The interpretation said less about Evelyn than about the hunger of a generation seeking symbols for its own questions.

The decade's political violence also shaped how her image was read. As television beamed images of assassinations and soldiers dying in Vietnam into living rooms, Evelyn's photograph resurfaced as part of a wider meditation on death in public space. Writers compared her serene repose to the bodies of protesters struck down by police, to students lying on campuses after clashes with the National Guard. The juxtaposition lent her image new power, transforming it from private despair into public allegory.

For antiwar activists, the photograph became another piece of evidence that America's triumphalist surface masked inner rot. "The most beautiful suicide," they said bitterly, was not a compliment but a condemnation: a nation that could not care for its daughters had no business exporting its ideals abroad.

Warhol's appropriation of Evelyn in his *Suicide* series coincided with these debates, amplifying the tension between fascination and exploitation. To his critics, his silkscreens multiplied her death into commodity, stripping it of dignity. To his admirers, he revealed the voyeurism already inherent in the photograph, forcing audiences to see their own complicity in turning tragedy into spectacle.

In galleries, viewers stood before the repeating images — Evelyn again and again, frozen at the moment after her leap — and felt both attraction and unease. The repetition dulled emotion even as it magnified it, making her at once unforgettable and strangely abstract. She was no longer Evelyn McHale, bookkeeper and fiancée. She was an icon, endlessly reproduced.

College students, restless and skeptical, sometimes claimed Evelyn as one of their own — not literally, but symbolically. Her leap became, for some, a rejection of the society they despised: materialism, conformity, hypocrisy. For young women especially, her act hovered as both warning and mirror. Some whispered that they understood her despair, that the weight of roles left little room for choice. Others recoiled, insisting that the women's movement was precisely about preventing such tragedies from repeating.

By the end of the 1960s, Evelyn McHale's image had been stretched across movements, philosophies, and protests she had never known. She was claimed as feminist prelude, existential parable, antiwar symbol, Pop Art icon. Each interpretation widened her reach — but also buried her voice.

The young woman who once kept ledgers in Manhattan, who feared she could not make a good wife, who kissed Barry goodbye at the station — she was harder and harder to see. The culture had claimed her, but in claiming her, it had erased her.

Chapter 26:

A Resurrection in Retrospect

By the 1970s, the photograph of Evelyn McHale was no longer a cutting from a magazine passed hand to hand. It had entered archives, anthologies, retrospectives. Photography itself underwent reevaluation, shifting from journalism to art, from documentation to interpretation. In this climate, Evelyn returned — not as the young woman who had leapt in 1947, but as an emblem reinterpreted by a new generation.

Major museums began to host exhibitions of twentieth-century photography, placing images of war, famine, and protest alongside portraits and street scenes. Among them, curators occasionally included Evelyn's photograph. Visitors stood before it, startled at how quiet it seemed amid the chaos of other images. Unlike the brutality of combat photography, Evelyn's stillness invited contemplation rather than recoil. Critics called it "a masterpiece of accidental composition," though the accident was a young woman's life.

Photography anthologies reproduced the image as well, labeling it "iconic." Students of visual culture dissected its lines, contrasts, and textures. Few anthologies included Evelyn's note. Fewer still mentioned Barry. The woman herself continued to vanish behind the photograph.

Second-wave feminism brought new critiques. Scholars argued that calling her death "the most beautiful suicide" reflected not Evelyn but the culture's need to aestheticize female suffering. "Had she been disfigured," one critic noted sharply, "the photograph would have been discarded. It was her beauty — her conformity to standards of femininity even in death — that allowed her to be remembered."

Feminist essays reframed her not as tragic muse but as victim of a society that silenced women's despair. The note's line — *"I wouldn't make a good wife for anybody"* — was revisited as both confession and indictment. It revealed the suffocating expectation that a woman's worth was tied solely to her marital role. In this reading, Evelyn was no longer "beautiful." She was testimony.

Meanwhile, the Cold War deepened. In the 1980s, amid renewed nuclear tensions, artists rediscovered Evelyn as symbol of fragility beneath power. Her leap from the Empire State Building, captured so serenely, was juxtaposed with images of mushroom clouds and missile silos. For some, she embodied the human face of despair in an age obsessed with annihilation.

Andy Warhol's earlier silkscreens of her image resurfaced in galleries, now viewed through the lens of irony and critique. Where the 1960s had debated voyeurism, the 1980s saw commodification itself as spectacle. Evelyn was consumed again, not only as symbol but as product: her face silk-screened, auctioned, reproduced in catalogs.

Through it all, the McHale family remained silent. By then, Barry had remarried quietly, though those close to him said he never fully let go of the memory of Evelyn. Her siblings built ordinary lives, avoiding the subject when journalists called. They did not attend exhibitions. They did not grant interviews. For them, Evelyn's persistence in culture was a reopening of wounds that had never healed.

171

Yet silence did not erase her from the public imagination. Each decade found new ways to resurrect her, new interpretations to impose, new contexts to fold her into. The private grief of family and fiancé had been overwhelmed by the cultural machinery of memory.

By the close of the 1980s, Evelyn McHale was no longer just the subject of one photograph. She was an icon of the twentieth century, her image migrating across disciplines — art, feminism, Cold War critique — each claiming her for its own purposes. But beneath all the interpretations, one truth remained constant: the woman herself was lost, reduced to a single moment captured on film, forever serene, forever silent.

Chapter 27:

The Digital Resurrection

By the 1990s, Evelyn McHale's photograph had already become a fixture in photography anthologies, art retrospectives, and feminist critiques. But as the century neared its close, a new force began reshaping memory: the digital archive. With the rise of image databases, online forums, and eventually the vast reach of the internet, Evelyn's face found yet another afterlife.

Photography publishers in the 1990s released thick, glossy books cataloging the "100 Most Iconic Photographs of the Twentieth Century."

Evelyn was nearly always there, nestled between the mushroom cloud over Hiroshima and the sailor kissing a nurse in Times Square. In these pages, she was presented as part of history's visual shorthand — instantly recognizable, endlessly reinterpreted.

For casual readers, her story was summarized in captions: *"The Most Beautiful Suicide — Evelyn McHale leapt from the Empire State Building in 1947. She was 23."* These lines distilled her life into a soundbite, her complexity erased in favor of a haunting image paired with a few stark facts.

As the 1990s gave way to the 2000s, Evelyn reemerged in a new medium: online forums and early websites devoted to dark curiosities. Her photograph, scanned from books or clipped from archives, spread across digital landscapes with a speed unimaginable in 1947.

Users debated the same paradox that had haunted critics for decades: how could death look so peaceful? Some shared the image with reverence, others with morbid fascination. A few added fragments of her note, stripped of context, as though they were poetry rather than the final words of a woman in despair.

In online communities dedicated to photography, Evelyn was admired for the "perfection of composition." In darker corners of the internet, she became part of galleries of death, her image stripped of respect and used as shock or spectacle. The photograph, once the property of *Life* magazine and art curators, was now freely copied, cropped, filtered, remixed.

The internet accelerated myth-making. Stories circulated that Evelyn had leapt on her wedding day, that she was a model, that she had been driven to despair by a scandalous affair. None of these were true. But in the churn of digital culture, truth mattered less than fascination. Evelyn had become folklore — her real life blurred by rumor, her real words drowned by invention.

Some online writers tried to correct the myths, publishing careful retellings of her story, quoting her note, situating her in the context of postwar America. Yet the myths persisted, spreading faster than corrections could keep up. The photograph had long since escaped the boundaries of history; online, it became whatever viewers wanted it to be.

For a new generation raised on screens, Evelyn was discovered not in museums or libraries but on message boards, blogs, and later social media feeds. Teenagers, scrolling late at night, stumbled across her serene face on the crushed limousine and felt compelled to pause. Some saw her as tragic, others as strangely inspiring, still others as merely uncanny. For them, she was not a relic of 1947 but an eternal figure, reappearing whenever curiosity pulled her image into circulation again.

By the early 2000s, Evelyn McHale had lived three lives: first as a daughter, fiancée, and bookkeeper; then as a cultural symbol in art and Cold War commentary; and finally as a digital myth, endlessly reproduced in pixels, endlessly misinterpreted.

She had leapt once from the Empire State Building, but the photograph of that leap had fallen again and again, landing in magazines, galleries, lecture halls, and now on glowing screens across the globe.

In life, she had feared she could not be a good wife. In death, she became something she had never wanted: unforgettable.

Chapter 28:

The Aesthetic of Melancholy

By the 2010s, Evelyn McHale's photograph was everywhere and nowhere at once. It surfaced not in museums alone, but on glowing screens: reposted on Tumblr mood boards, filtered and re-filtered on Instagram, embedded in YouTube montages of "haunting photographs." She had become part of a digital canon of sadness, her image drifting through feeds and timelines alongside black-and-white portraits of James Dean, Sylvia Plath, and Billie Holiday.

On Tumblr, Evelyn's photograph appeared beneath captions like *"there is beauty in brokenness"* or *"she was too delicate for this world.* " Stripped of context, the image became raw material for a global aesthetic of melancholy, one that equated fragility with authenticity. Teenagers in bedrooms across the world reblogged the photograph, pairing it with lyrics, fragments of poetry, and their own whispered confessions.

Few included Evelyn's note. Fewer still mentioned Barry Rhodes, her family, or the cultural weight of 1947. Online, she was timeless — a symbol of despair unmoored from history. To some, she was an icon of resistance, a woman who rejected the roles forced upon her. To others, she was a romantic figure, enshrined in the same mythic aura that once surrounded doomed poets and tragic starlets.

On Instagram, her face and folded hands resurfaced in curated feeds devoted to "dark aesthetics." Some users posted the photograph beside images of abandoned buildings, storm clouds, or neon-lit alleys, weaving her into collages of urban alienation. Hashtags like #tragicbeauty and #lostsouls linked her to an entire subculture of curated sadness.

Here, too, truth blurred. Captions sometimes misidentified her as a bride who leapt on her wedding day, or as a model crushed by scandal. Myths traveled faster than corrections. To question them was almost irrelevant: the image mattered more than the history.

On YouTube, compilations of "history's most haunting photographs" often began or ended with Evelyn. Set to minor-key piano or whispered narration, the image was presented as evidence of life's fragility. Comment sections filled with responses: *"She looks like she's sleeping." "The saddest photo I've ever seen." "I hope she's at peace."*

Others argued, angrily, about whether sharing the image was exploitative or necessary. The debates echoed those of 1947, of the 1960s, of the 1980s — proof that each generation rediscovered Evelyn anew, repeating the same questions without resolution.

What united these digital reincarnations was their focus not on Evelyn's life, but on her *image*. She was rarely discussed as a person — a 23-year-old bookkeeper, a fiancée, a daughter shaped by family fractures and postwar pressures. She was consumed instead as mood, as symbol, as aesthetic shorthand for despair.

And yet, for countless individuals scrolling late at night, her face offered a strange form of connection. Some felt less alone seeing her serenity, even if they misunderstood its cause. Others whispered in comments that they, too, felt crushed by expectation, by silence, by roles they could not bear. Evelyn had not intended to become comfort for strangers. But in the digital age, her image became precisely that: a mirror into which others projected their own loneliness.

By the 2010s, Evelyn McHale had become part of the endless churn of internet culture. She was reblogged, reposted, remixed, reframed — timeless but rootless, forever serene, forever falling.

Her leap had lasted seconds. Her photograph, now, lasted forever.

Chapter 29:

The Present Haunting

More than seventy years after Evelyn McHale's leap, her face remains everywhere — in glossy photography books, in academic lectures, in Tumblr archives that refuse to vanish, in Instagram feeds curated for mood rather than memory. She endures as one of the most circulated images of the twentieth century, though she never chose to be.

In the age of podcasts and streaming media, Evelyn's story has been retold countless times. True crime shows, history podcasts, and cultural commentary series feature episodes about her, each with its own framing: *"The Most Beautiful Suicide," "The Girl on the Limo," "The Photograph That Stopped Time."* Some treat her respectfully, lingering on her note, her family, her fiancé. Others sensationalize her, emphasizing spectacle over substance. Listeners, earbuds in, carry her story on subway rides and walks through city streets — Evelyn retold in voices she never knew, for audiences she never imagined.

Writers in the 2020s revisit Evelyn's image with new urgency. Essays in digital magazines interrogate the ethics of circulation. Is it exploitation to continue reproducing the photograph? Is it voyeurism to linger on her serene face, knowing the violence of her death? Some argue that the image serves as a warning, forcing society to confront the cost of silence around mental health. Others argue that by aestheticizing despair, it risks romanticizing suicide.

The debates echo those of 1947, 1960, of 1980 — yet each time they feel urgent, because Evelyn's photograph will not release its grip on the cultural imagination.

In the twenty-first century, her story also collides with growing awareness of mental health. Advocates cite her as evidence of how far society has come — and how far it has yet to go. In 1947, Evelyn's depression and doubts were unspoken, her fears of becoming her mother a private torment. Today, discussions of anxiety, depression, and generational trauma are more public. Yet her image still unsettles: a reminder of what happens when silence outweighs voice.

Perhaps the most persistent question is whether it is right to look at Evelyn at all. The photograph is undeniably powerful, undeniably haunting. But to gaze upon it is to participate in a chain of voyeurism that began the moment Robert Wiles lifted his camera. Some argue that art demands we look, that truth cannot be sanitized. Others counter that Evelyn deserved dignity, that her final act should not be consumed endlessly as aesthetic object.

This debate plays out in classrooms, in online comment threads, in museum halls where her photograph sometimes hangs. Visitors lean in, studying her folded hands, her calm face, her skirt lying neatly amid shattered glass. They whisper the same words spoken for decades: *"She looks like she's sleeping." "It's so beautiful." "It doesn't look real."*

But it was real.

In the 2020s, Evelyn lives on in fragments: in essays, in pixels, in lectures, in whispers. She is claimed by feminists as evidence, by artists as icon, by melancholic teens as muse, by historians as case study. Each claim pulls her further from herself.

And yet, despite all the distortions, one truth persists: Evelyn was a young woman who felt she could not live the life the world demanded of her. The photograph may have transformed her into symbol, but behind it was silence, and within the silence was a person.

Evelyn McHale leapt from the Empire State Building in 1947. She leapt once, but she has been falling ever since — through art, through culture, through history, through screens. A single photograph ensures that she will never land fully in peace. She remains suspended, haunting the imagination of each generation that rediscovers her.

Chapter 30:

The Woman and the Image

The story of Evelyn McHale began long before May 1, 1947, but for the world, it always begins there — with a fall, a limousine, and a photograph. It is tempting to end it the same way, to let the image stand as conclusion. Yet to stop there would be to betray her, to allow the myth to eclipse the woman.

She was not only the serene figure on the crumpled car. She was a child shaped by her mother's instability, a daughter navigating fractured loyalties, a sister, a friend. She was a bookkeeper who balanced ledgers with quiet precision.

She was a fiancée who kissed Barry goodbye with a calm smile. She was a woman who felt the weight of roles she could not inhabit, who feared a future that seemed to close around her like walls.

In her note, she offered no poetry, no flourish. Only honesty: *"I wouldn't make a good wife for anybody."* These words, plain and stark, reveal more than any caption or essay. They were not the script of a tragic heroine. They were the confession of a young woman caught between silence and expectation, believing she could not live within either.

The photograph transformed that confession into spectacle. It froze her not in pain but in poise, not in despair but in serenity. It allowed strangers to call her beautiful, to project meaning onto her, to fold her into debates about art, gender, politics, and mortality. Each generation rediscovered her, remade her, claimed her. But in each retelling, the person receded.

Barry carried her privately, her family mourned her quietly, but the culture consumed her endlessly. She became lesson, symbol, icon.

And yet beneath the layers of interpretation, the truth remains painfully simple: Evelyn McHale was human. She struggled. She faltered. She could not find space in a world that offered her no words for her despair.

Perhaps the greatest tragedy is not only her leap but what followed: the transformation of her life into an image that could never rest. For decades, she has fallen again and again — from magazine pages, from gallery walls, from digital feeds — her body serene, her silence echoing.

And yet, to look at Evelyn is also to be reminded of our own responsibility. To ask what stories we tell about despair, what roles we force upon others, what silences we ignore until they become unbearable. To look at her is to be haunted not by beauty, but by the cost of indifference.

In the end, the woman and the image cannot be reconciled. The image will remain, endlessly reproduced, endlessly misinterpreted. But the woman — Evelyn — lived once, loved once, despaired once.

She deserves to be remembered not only for how she died, but for the complexity of how she lived.

The Empire State Building still rises above New York, indifferent and gleaming. The limousine long ago was towed away, repaired or discarded. The crowds who gathered that morning are gone, their whispers vanished. But the photograph remains, a shard of time that refuses to fade.

And Evelyn remains within it — not as muse, not as myth, but as reminder. Behind every image is a life. Behind every symbol, a human being. Behind every silence, a voice that once longed to be heard.

Epilogue:

The Weight of Silence

Evelyn Francis McHale was born into a family already cracked. A father whose sternness concealed his own wounds, a mother whose instability cast long shadows over the household, siblings scattered by circumstance. From the beginning, she learned that composure was survival, that silence could shield her from chaos.

As she grew, she perfected that silence. At work, she was diligent, precise, and efficient. With friends, she was kind but reserved. With Barry, she was affectionate but measured, giving him smiles and reassurance while keeping her doubts folded inside. To all who knew her, she seemed steady, poised, the sort of young woman who could step into marriage and fulfill the role her era demanded.

But inside, Evelyn carried the memory of her mother's unraveling, the fear that the same fate lived in her veins. When she wrote, *"Tell my father, I too much of my mother's tendency,"* she confessed what she had never dared to say aloud: that she feared she was broken in a way that love could not mend.

The culture of her time offered no refuge for such fears. In 1947, women were urged to return to kitchens, to embrace domesticity, to measure their worth by their husbands' satisfaction. Magazines sold them recipes and beauty tips but gave no language for despair. Psychologists of the day spoke of "maladjustment," not trauma. Silence was the prescription. Silence was the cage.

Evelyn lived in that silence until it became unbearable. She believed she could not be a good wife, and because marriage was the measure of her era, she believed she could not be good at all.

The choice she made was not sudden but cumulative — the product of a lifetime of quiet fears, unspoken doubts, cultural scripts that left no space for deviation.

When she climbed the railing of the Empire State Building's observation deck, she was not rebelling against Barry alone, nor against her father, nor even against herself. She was stepping out of a world that had never given her room to be imperfect, to be fragile, to be human.

The photograph that followed — Robert Wiles's accidental masterpiece — froze her into myth. The world saw beauty where she had felt despair, serenity where she had carried silence. Each generation thereafter remade her, projecting onto her face its own anxieties, its own fascinations. She became "the most beautiful suicide," a phrase that both immortalized and erased her.

But behind the image was a woman, and behind the woman were the products of life that led her there:

- A childhood fractured by her mother's instability and her father's distance.

- A culture that demanded women smile through silence and measure themselves by marriage.

- A society that aestheticized beauty but ignored pain.

- An age that celebrated progress while leaving individuals alone with their despair.

Evelyn was not a symbol of failure, nor a prophet of liberation. She was a human being pressed against limits that offered her no way forward. Her leap was not into beauty, nor into history, nor into art. But it was into *release*.

What remains is not only a photograph, but a question — how many silences still weigh upon us, how many lives remain unseen until they end? Evelyn's tragedy is not only that she died, but that she lived in a world that could not hear her.

And so, the photograph endures — haunting, unforgettable, endlessly interpreted. But to honor Evelyn is to remember the life behind the image, the quiet woman who feared she could not be what the world demanded, who deserved not myth but understanding.

The Empire State Building still gleams in the New York skyline, indifferent, magnificent. Crowds still gather at its railings, gazing outward at the city's vastness. Few remember the young woman who once stood there, gloves folded neatly, skirt smoothed, before stepping into the void.

But if we remember her at all, let it be not for her beauty in death, but for the silence she carried in life — and the lesson that silence, left unspoken, can weigh more than anyone should bear.

The Cultural Significance of Evelyn McHale's Death

On May 1, 1947, twenty-three-year-old Evelyn McHale leapt from the Empire State Building's 86th-floor observation deck, landing on the roof of a United Nations limousine. Her act of despair might have remained a tragic footnote in New York City's history had it not been captured by photography student Robert Wiles. The photograph, later published in *Life* magazine, immortalized McHale's serene pose amid the violence of her fall. Critics, journalists, and artists dubbed it "the most beautiful suicide." Over the decades, McHale's image has transcended her individual story, becoming a cultural symbol that reflects postwar gender dynamics, urban alienation, Cold War anxieties, and the continuing tension between voyeurism and art. This essay explores the cultural significance of McHale's death, situating it within broader historical and social contexts while considering its enduring presence in art, feminist critique, and digital culture.

Photography and the Creation of an Icon

The single most important factor in the cultural afterlife of Evelyn McHale was the photograph itself. As Susan Sontag (1977) argued, photography does not merely record reality but frames and interprets it. Wiles's image transformed a violent suicide into a tableau of serenity: McHale's hands folded, her face calm, her skirt unruffled, as though she were peacefully asleep. The juxtaposition between her composed appearance and the twisted steel beneath her body imbued the image with a haunting paradox. Published in *Life* magazine on May 12, 1947, the photograph reached millions of readers, ensuring McHale's leap would not vanish into obscurity (Goldberg, 1991).

The circulation of the photograph established McHale as a visual icon. Unlike countless other suicides, hers became part of cultural memory because it was aestheticized. This raises ethical questions: was the beauty ascribed to her image a form of respect, or was it exploitation of her despair? Scholars such as Batchen (2004) note that the framing of death through photography often shifts the focus from the subject's humanity to the audience's fascination. In McHale's case, the image quickly eclipsed her lived reality, reducing her to a symbol of "tragic beauty."

Postwar Gender Roles and the Feminine Ideal

McHale's suicide note read, in part: *"He is much better off without me. I wouldn't make a good wife for anybody."* These words cannot be disentangled from the cultural climate of 1947. Following World War II, American society encouraged women to leave wartime jobs and return to domestic roles. Advertisements, magazines, and policy reinforced the ideal of the suburban housewife as the pinnacle of feminine fulfillment (May, 1988).

For women like McHale, whose self-worth was measured against the expectation of marriage and homemaking, doubts about her suitability as a wife could translate into an overwhelming sense of failure.

Betty Friedan's (1963) later description of "the problem that has no name" resonates with McHale's despair. Women were urged to find contentment in domesticity, yet many experienced dissatisfactions that society silenced. McHale's note suggests she internalized this pressure to the point of despair, fearing she could not live up to the feminine ideal. Feminist scholars interpret her death as emblematic of the invisible burdens placed on women in mid-century America (Faludi, 1991). In this sense, McHale's leap represents not only a personal tragedy but also the crushing weight of gender conformity.

Urban Alienation and Modernity

Beyond gender, McHale's death was framed as a symbol of urban alienation. Falling from the Empire State Building — the tallest skyscraper of its time and a monument to modern ambition — her body resting on a limousine for diplomats seemed almost allegorical.

Sociologists connected her act to Émile Durkheim's (1897/1951) concept of anomie, the breakdown of social norms that leaves individuals feeling disconnected and purposeless.

The image thus embodied contradictions of postwar modernity: prosperity coexisted with loneliness; technological triumph towered over fragile lives. As historian Jackson (2003) notes, postwar cities often symbolized both opportunity and despair, promising anonymity and freedom but also producing alienation. McHale's leap literalized this tension, making her a figure through which critics could question the costs of modern urban life.

Cold War Ideological Appropriations

In the international context, McHale's image was reframed through Cold War politics. Soviet commentators used the photograph as evidence of capitalist emptiness, arguing that America's skyscrapers masked inner despair (Dobrenko & Naiman, 2003). French existentialists, influenced by Sartre and Camus, read her leap as confrontation with the absurd: a moment when freedom becomes unbearable (Camus, 1942/1991). British critics compared her serene repose to the stoicism of wartime civilians, interpreting her death as emblem of dignity amid despair.

Each interpretation projected national anxieties onto McHale. She became, unwillingly, a mirror in which cultures saw their own contradictions: capitalist alienation, existential absurdity, or the fragility of postwar optimism. Her personal story vanished beneath these ideological appropriations.

Artistic Afterlife: From Warhol to the Digital Age

The 1960s and beyond cemented McHale as an artistic symbol. Andy Warhol incorporated her image into his *Suicide* series, multiplying her photograph into silkscreens that underscored the commodification of death (Crow, 1996). Poets and novelists invoked her as muse or metaphor, often romanticizing her despair. By the late twentieth century, her image was included in anthologies of "iconic" photographs, ensuring her place in visual culture.

The rise of digital media gave her image yet another afterlife. On Tumblr, Instagram, and YouTube, the photograph circulated as part of an "aesthetic of melancholy." Users paired it with song lyrics or poetry, transforming McHale into a symbol of fragility or rebellion. Yet these digital appropriations often perpetuated myths — that she was a bride, a model, or a glamorous celebrity — erasing her true identity as a bookkeeper and fiancée.

As Gunning (2008) suggests, the internet accelerates the decontextualization of images, turning history into endlessly recycled fragments. McHale's photograph, stripped of context, became timeless but rootless, a visual shorthand for despair detached from the specifics of her life.

The Ethics of Looking

The persistent fascination with McHale's death raises ethical dilemmas. Is it voyeurism to continue reproducing the photograph? Or is it necessary to confront despair through the visual record? Sontag (2003) argued that images of suffering simultaneously provoke empathy and aestheticize pain, placing viewers in a morally ambiguous position. McHale's photograph embodies this tension: it compels attention while risking romanticization.

Mental health advocates warn that the romantic framing of suicide as "beautiful" can be dangerous, potentially influencing vulnerable individuals (Joiner, 2005). At the same time, her story underscores the importance of recognizing silent despair. The cultural afterlife of her image reveals society's struggle to balance respect for the individual with fascination for the spectacle of death.

Enduring Legacy

Evelyn McHale's death endures not simply because it was tragic, but because it intersected with larger cultural currents: postwar gender roles, urban alienation, Cold War politics, and the aestheticization of despair. Her image continues to provoke debate in art, psychology, feminism, and digital culture. Each generation rediscovers her, projects new meaning onto her, and in doing so reveals its own anxieties.

Yet perhaps the truest cultural significance of McHale's death lies in its reminder of the cost of silence. She was a young woman who feared she could not live up to expectations, who carried private doubts without outlet, who found release only in a leap from the tallest tower of her time. Her photograph immortalized her, but it also obscured her humanity. To honor her now requires not only looking at the image, but listening to the silence that preceded it.

Conclusion

The photograph of Evelyn McHale is one of the most enduring images of the twentieth century. It has been celebrated as art, critiqued as exploitation, and recycled as digital folklore. Its cultural significance lies in the way it became a mirror for postwar America and beyond, reflecting fears of gender confinement, modern alienation, and ideological struggle. Yet at the core remains a simple, devastating truth: Evelyn was a young woman who despaired of a life she felt unable to live.

Her leap from the Empire State Building lasted seconds, but its resonance has lasted decades.

It forces us to ask not only why we remember her, but how we remember her — as an icon of beauty in death, or as a reminder of the silences we must learn to hear in life.

Author's Note

This book began with a photograph. A young woman lies upon a limousine roof, her hands folded, her face serene, her skirt neat despite the violence that carried her there. It is an image many of us have seen — in magazines, in anthologies, on the internet — but too often, it is consumed without context, as though beauty were explanation enough.

But behind every image is a life. Behind Evelyn McHale was a family fractured by illness and distance, a fiancé who loved her, and a culture that gave her no language for despair. She was not a myth or a muse. She was a woman who felt crushed by the weight of expectations

213

— to marry, to perform stability, to embody a role she feared she could not fulfill.

Evelyn's leap from the Empire State Building in 1947 was not simply a private act of despair. It was also shaped by her time: an America that demanded conformity, that silenced women's fears, that praised beauty while ignoring pain. The products of her life — fractured family, cultural scripts, and an era that offered no safe space for vulnerability — converged into the moment of her death.

This book does not seek to glorify Evelyn's choice, nor to aestheticize her despair. Rather, it seeks to restore her humanity, to peel back the layers of myth that have accumulated around a single photograph. To see her not only as the subject of an image, but as a person with doubts, silences, and longings that remain heartbreakingly familiar today.

Evelyn's story endures because it confronts us with questions we still face. How do we listen to the silences of those around us? How do we resist the cultural pressures that measure worth by appearance, role, or conformity? How do we honor individuals not for how they died, but for the fullness of their lives?

In remembering Evelyn McHale, we are reminded of the cost of silence. Her image may remain suspended in time, but her lesson is not about beauty in death. It is about the necessity of giving voice to despair before it becomes unbearable.

May this book stand not only as a narrative of one woman's life, but also as a call to see — and to listen — more deeply, so that no one need to leap into silence to be heard.

Wayne J. Gombar

References

Batchen, G. (2004). *Forget me not: Photography and remembrance*. Princeton Architectural Press.

Camus, A. (1991). *The myth of Sisyphus* (J. O'Brien, Trans.). Vintage International. (Original work published 1942)

Crow, T. (1996). *Modern art in the common culture*. Yale University Press.

Dobrenko, E., & Naiman, E. (Eds.). (2003). *The landscape of Stalinism: The art and ideology of Soviet space*. University of Washington Press.

Durkheim, É. (1951). *Suicide: A study in sociology* (J. Spaulding & G. Simpson, Trans.). Free Press. (Original work published 1897)

Faludi, S. (1991). *Backlash: The undeclared war against American women*. Crown Publishing.

Friedan, B. (1963). *The feminine mystique*. W. W. Norton.

Goldberg, V. (1991). *The power of photography: How photographs changed our lives*. Abbeville Press.

Gunning, T. (2008). What's the point of an index? Or, Faking photographs. *Nordicom Review, 29*(2), 39–49.

Jackson, K. T. (2003). *The encyclopedia of New York City*. Yale University Press.

Joiner, T. (2005). *Why people die by suicide*. Harvard University Press.

May, E. T. (1988). *Homeward bound: American families in the Cold War era*. Basic Books.

Sontag, S. (1977). *On photography*. Farrar, Straus and Giroux.

Sontag, S. (2003). *Regarding the pain of others*. Farrar, Straus and Giroux.

Made in United States
North Haven, CT
08 December 2025

84044049R00124